A Fun & Care Book

DOGS!

For Today's Pet Owner
From the Publishers of DOGFANCY Magazine

Lynette Padwa and Lani Scheman

photographs by Reneé Stockdale

BOWTIE™
P R E S S

Irvine, California

Cover photograph courtesy of Robin Buckley

Information on pages 41-43 was adapted from "How to Choose the Pick of the Litter," by Liz Palika
(*Dog Fancy,* April 1994, pp. 41-43).

Information in the sidebar on page 35 was adapted from "Buying a Puppy," by Susan Lacroix Hamil
(*Dog Fancy*, April 1995, p. 59).

The dogs in this book are referred to as *he* or *she* in alternating chapters unless
their gender is apparent from the activity discussed.

Ruth Berman, editor-in-chief
Nick Clemente, special consultant
Yumi Oshima, designer

Library of Congress Cataloging-in-Publication Data

Padwa Lynette.
    Dogs! : for today's pet owner from the publishers of Dog fancy
magazine / Lynette Padwa, Lani Scheman ; photographs by Reneé
Stockdale.
       p.   cm. -- (A Fun & care book)
    Includes bibliographical references (p.   ) and index.
    ISBN 1-889540-03-X
    1. Dogs.   I. Scheman, Lani, 1955-   . II. Title.   III. Series.
SF426.P28   1998
636.7--dc21   97-32166
                                                                         CIP

BowTie™ Press
3 Burroughs
Irvine, California 92618

Manufactured in the United States of America

First Printing April 1998

10 9 8 7 6 5 4 3 2 1

Acknowledgments

Many thanks to Ruth Berman, Nick Clemente, and Bonnie Lund for their help and encouragement.

L.P.

I would like to thank my good friend, Lynette Padwa, and Ruth Berman for the opportunity to work on this book.

L.S.

I would like to thank breeders Annie & Ron Cogo-Windfall (Labradors); Nancy Chargo-Banner (Labradors); Pauline Mortier-Lubberline (Labradors); Barb & Ed Scully-Boos' Bulldog Farm; Diane Rissman, Pamala & Heath Sallows (Mid-Michigan Pug Club). Thanks to Lorena Heiniger, Louise Moore, and Bailey from the Evangelical Home; Humane Society of Huron Valley; Capital Area Humane Society; Mellissa Hernly and the Obedience Training Club of Greater Lansing; Jenny Zablotony (Newfie Rescue); Heart of Michigan Bernese Mountain Dog Club. Thanks also to cover models Michelle Nawrocki and Buddy and models Jan and Johnny Grunt and Toby and Tawny; Joan Giannola and Heida; Marti and Myia Blackwood; Kelly Quigley and Yukon; Linda Ziehm, Katie Colby, and Breeze; Jenny Clark; Patti Tuck and Speckles; Drs. Lori DeGrazia and Kirt Henkel (and Kiwi); Amy McDonald; Nancy and Nicole Mitts; Brian Shelby and Ashlee; Robin, Jake, and Trevor Meinicki; Janet Talbot and Little Dog, Vicki Crilly and Hoss. I would also like to thank my husband and son for their love and support AND for putting up with puppy poop!

To Grampa & Buck, may they both be in peace.

R.S.

Contents

Dogs and People: A Natural History

Dogs are much more than "man's best friend." They are also our oldest friends, companions who have curled up at our feet since the Paleolithic era. We marvel at their empathy, playfulness, and ability to read our moods, yet we shouldn't be surprised; for thousands of years we humans have been encouraging dogs to have just these traits. We have selectively bred them to be the perfect pets, and in turn they have become both devoted to and dependent upon us. Over the millennia, canines and humans have grown up together, and that may be why a dog's companionship feels so familiar and comforting to us.

Cave dwellers in what is now Iraq shared their food and shelter with domesticated dogs 14,000 years ago. Elsewhere around the world—in southern Europe, Denmark, North America, and China—there is evidence that dogs were serving as guards or companions at least 10,000 years back. There's little doubt that by that time, the lives of dogs and people were already thoroughly enmeshed. Were these canines similar to the household pets we know today? In all likelihood, the answer is yes. Although dogs share similarities with other canids such as wolves and jackals, dogs have distinct characteristics that set them apart from their wilder cousins. To an astonishing degree, these distinctions are a result of their contact with human beings. Across the globe, humans domesticated wild canids and bred them to emphasize specific traits, such as docility, that are desirable in domestic pets. Part of your pet's personality is born of her wild ancestors, while another part is ingrained from centuries of tutelage at a master's feet.

Wild Dogs and Domestic Dogs

Much research has gone into trying to discover the true progenitors of dogs. Did domestic dogs descend from wolves, jackals, foxes, coyotes, dingoes, or perhaps another kind of wild dog? Experts have no clear answer to the question, and some of them now believe that domestic dogs are a combination of all of these animals, with the possible exception of the fox, who behaves quite differently from other canids. Wherever humans have roamed, they appear to have taken in pups from the local canid population, raised them, and bred those individuals with pleasant or useful characteristics.

All canids (with the exception of foxes) share certain traits that you can easily see reflected in your own family dog. The most obvious of these is their sociability. If given the

Above: *The domestic dog probably descended from several types of wild dogs, including the wolf.*

Right: *You can read the body language of these dogs. The golden retriever on top is asserting dominance over the submissive-acting lab mix.*

opportunity, all dogs live and hunt in organized packs and follow a strict dominance hierarchy. The pack members are loyal to their leader and to each other, and will nurture the puppies, whether or not they are the actual parents.

Wild and domestic dogs use the same body language to communicate fear, anger, dominance, and submission. Both share the ability to howl, bark, and yip, although dogs in the wild rarely bark. Wild or domesticated, dogs bury bones and food and return to them later, roll in foul-smelling refuse, and mark their territory with urine.

Every dog owner is familiar with the curious, sometimes exasperating habit dogs have of sniffing and spraying every tree and fire hydrant they pass on their daily walk. In the wild, too, canids pick out certain trees and large rocks to serve as the neighborhood bulletin board. Each passing dog leaves his or her mark for the other dogs to sniff. Some experts believe that a wealth of information is contained in these scents, including the dog's age, sex, health, and perhaps her most recent meal. Even more intriguing is the possibility that the scent carries emotional information as well, with clues as to whether the animal was frightened, happy, or sexually available.

Both domestic and wild dogs instinctively mark their territories with urine.

Dogs in the wild and domesticated dogs have many physical similarities, too. For example, German shepherds, malamutes, Samoyeds, huskies, and collies, to name only a few, look very much like wolves. But wolves' eyes have oval pupils, which give them a much different countenance than dogs, whose round pupils somehow seem more human. Jackals and coyotes look very doglike, being lighter and smaller than most wolves. Dingoes and other wild dogs are also extremely similar to domestic dogs, except that their ears are always pricked and their faces are triangular, with a flat brow. Both wild and domestic dogs have a large chest and narrow waist. They all have an acute sense of smell, hearing, and eyesight, although their color vision is limited. With the possible exception of the fox, all the canids can interbreed. Where, then, does the wild dog end and the domestic dog begin?

The Domestication of Dogs

Fourteen thousand years is a long time for a breeding program. Over the course of history, humans have left their mark on dogs, both physically and behaviorally, by breeding those who had certain desirable characteristics—a process called selective breeding. The result is that no matter how many traits domestic dogs may share with their wild relatives, the two are fundamentally different. Humans have bred dogs to be agreeable, dependent, and docile—more like puppies than adult wild dogs—so that they would be more likely to make pleasant pets. This breeding for puppylike characteristics is called neoteny, and it applies to physical as well as behavioral traits.

Our ancestors were no doubt very concerned that their canine companions behave civilly around the hearth. Overly aggressive dogs, who would challenge humans, were a danger to children, who were sure to be the aggressive dogs' first victims. Docile, submissive dogs were bred to each other to create breeds that are dependent on humans the way puppies are dependent on their mothers. This dependency is relative; a docile, dependent dog doesn't necessarily whimper and roll over but tolerates human beings and forms a bond with us. In other words, dogs are tractable, affectionate animals.

As humans were breeding dogs to be friendly and obedient, they also attempted to eliminate the wild dogs' natural fear of new situations and unfamiliar creatures. Anxious, fearful dogs are not all that uncommon even today, and people are still attempting to eradicate those traits through selective breeding.

Physically, humans also favored puppylike features in their adult dogs and bred them accordingly. This meant selecting smaller dogs; those with shorter, blunter, more puppylike muzzles; and dogs with floppy ears as opposed to upright, pricked ears. (In the wild, all dogs have pricked ears, but some wild pups have floppy ears.) We humans derive aesthetic pleasure from color and variety, and to satisfy this urge we have bred dogs for their colorful or unusual coats. Most dogs in the wild have drab coats that are fairly uniform in length and density. Domestic breeds, on the other hand, boast an astounding variety of coat styles, from short or even hairless coats to long, ropy pelts or fur that is as sleek and soft as mink.

Early humans bred docile, submissive wild dogs who had puppylike features to create today's incredible variety of lovable companions.

Dog researchers have identified at least thirty-nine different canid species, one of which is the domestic dog, *Canis familiaris*. But *Canis familiaris* is composed of hundreds of breeds—the American Kennel Club (AKC) registers 143, and some experts place the worldwide number of breeds at more than 800.

Our massive breeding program has resulted in an inexhaustible selection of dogs to choose as companions or helpers. In addition to breeding canines to be puppylike and docile, over the centuries different groups of people have bred dogs to perform various useful tasks: herding, guarding, retrieving, tracking, and so forth. Many of these tasks grew directly out of the dog's use in the hunt.

A Partner for Hunt, Herd, and Hearth

On cave walls from Spain to Africa, researchers have found drawings of dogs hunting alongside humans. In some cases, it's not clear whether the dogs were part of a wild pack or were working in tandem with humans. But one painting discovered in the Atlas Mountains of northwestern Africa clearly depicts a hunter standing with his bow drawn, his dogs positioned behind him. That composition dates from around 3000 B.C., so we can be fairly certain that dogs were hunting with humans by that time.

Today, our relationship with dogs reflects thousands of years of shared history.

Dogs such as this German shepherd were bred to protect livestock and are capable of handling other challenging tasks as well.

Next to hunting, dogs in ancient times were employed mainly as guards. In Persia, they were valued above all other beasts as "the guardian of the flock and the defender of man"—one of the earliest references to dogs as shepherds. Dogs have a natural instinct to protect the pack, and early nomadic tribes put this tendency to use by training dogs to guard their flocks from predators. These early sheepdogs were formidable canines, able to ward off bears, wolves, and other wild animals. White or light-colored dogs were favored because they were easy to spot at night—or among a pack of wolves, should the herdsman have to help the dog keep marauders at bay.

From country to country, herdsmen bred sheepdogs suited to the terrain, the climate, and the type of livestock they were expected to guard. Sheepdogs are among the most intelligent of canines—Border collies (a type of sheepdog) are at the top of the canine intelligence charts—but their abilities have been put to real use only since the 1800s, when the threat of wild animals subsided. At that point, sheepdogs were trained for more challenging work such as finding lost animals and returning them to the fold.

Ancient cultures used dogs to guard not only livestock but people as well. The ancient Greeks stationed dogs outside their fortresses, relying on them to protect the town and raise the alarm should an enemy attack. The citadel of Corinth was the site of one remarkable defensive action on the part of guard dogs. There, while the army slept, fifty dogs posted outside the fortress defended Corinth against a surprise raid. All but one of these brave dogs perished. The remaining dog roused the soldiers, who eventually fended off the attack. The citizens of Corinth were so touched by the animals' heroism that they erected a marble monument to the memory of the forty-nine dogs who died that night. Soter, the surviving dog, was given a lifetime pension and a silver collar.

Dogs have always followed people into combat, and since earliest recorded history, they appear to have been bred for this purpose. As much as the Persians revered their sheepdogs, for instance, they didn't hesitate to send huge mastiffs off to war. In the sixth century B.C., Cyrus the Great ordered four towns in Babylon to breed mastiffs for the sole purpose of attacking prisoners and traitors.

Ancient cultures prized dogs as both hunters and companions. In China, evidence suggests that dogs were cherished as pets as early as 3468 B.C. Records show that during that era, the Chinese were already breeding tiny "sleeve dogs" who could be carried about inside the sleeves of their loose clothing.

Artifacts from around 2100 B.C. found in Egypt depict four types of canines that existed side by side with humans: greyhounds, mastiffs, a dog similar to the Australian dingo, and a smaller dog. By 1500 B.C., drawings of dogs began to appear in Egyptian tombs, a sign that the animals were treasured by their masters. In some respects, the Egyptians placed a far greater value on their dogs than we do today—killing a dog was punishable by death. However, in China and Egypt, as elsewhere around the world, the dog was still valued mainly as a hunter.

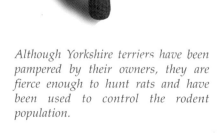

Although Yorkshire terriers have been pampered by their owners, they are fierce enough to hunt rats and have been used to control the rodent population.

The Breeds Expand

As civilizations evolved, breeds became more diversified. The noble classes were always looking to refine their hunting dogs by breeding them for specific types of prey. On a trip to the Holy Land, Louis IX (1214-1270) of France saw gray dogs used to hunt gazelles. Louis promptly imported some to France. Thereafter, Europeans continued to promote specialty dogs: Alan dogs (descendants of mastiffs) to hunt bears or wild boars; smaller bird dogs to startle grouse and partridge from

The first evidence of greyhounds was found on an Egyptian tomb dating to as early as 2900 B.C.

their cover; setters to "set," or flatten themselves against the ground so that hunters with nets could easily move around them; and hounds to tirelessly run down a stag or corner a wild boar. Greyhounds were the most prized of all canines, due to their terrific speed and strong jaws.

By the sixteenth century, the Germans were classifying hunting dogs: pointers, beaters, chasers, casters, and netting dogs were some of their categories. But the Renaissance saw a shift in peoples' attitudes toward dogs. Although they were still used to hunt and accompany men into battle, dogs had also become firmly entrenched in the hearts of men and women. Lapdogs—often of the Maltese, bichon frise, or Pomeranian breeds—were favored by wealthy Italian ladies, and fierce mastiffs were prized by their husbands. The enthusiasm for small dogs reached a fever pitch in France during the 1570s, when Henry III took to arriving in court wearing around his neck a small basket brimming with little dogs. In 1576, he spent 100,000 gold crowns pursuing his passion for dogs, and in 1578, he issued a decree declaring that water spaniels and hounds were no longer to be used for hunting. Commoners who disobeyed this law were put to death.

Toy breeds such as the English toy spaniel made their appearance during the 1600s; ladies of the English court delighted in the antics and soulfulness of these pets. Not only were dogs valued as amusing playmates for ladies of the court, they were also likely to be put to work in various innovative ways—turning a spit or performing tricks in the village square. As they had for hundreds of years, dogs in rural areas continued to tend flocks. But for the most part, hunting dogs still held center stage.

Dogs in the Modern World

The next several centuries saw an explosion in breeds across Europe, due in part to the French Revolution of 1789. The laws that made all citizens equal, freed commoners to hunt in the open country—an activity that formerly had been restricted to the noble classes. Dogs were essential to the hunt, but whereas noblemen preferred high-maintenance breeds such as Great Pyrenees, peasants required more humble dogs. The French, Germans, Italians, and Spanish began to breed hounds and spaniels, while the British concentrated on "gundogs" with deep chests and long limbs. The British fascination with breeding eventually produced a great variety of dogs, including setters and pointers.

Since the 1800s, a tremendous number of new breeds have been developed. In late-nineteenth-century England and Scotland, a new type of terrier seemed to sprout up every year, from snowy West Highland whites to Yorkshire terriers and magnificent Kerry blue terriers. The rest of Europe, too, became more interested in breeding dogs and showing off the results to fellow animal lovers.

In 1859, the first dog show was organized in England. The United States followed suit with a dog show in 1875. The dog shows spawned kennel clubs—the English Kennel Club in 1873, the American Kennel Club in 1884. From that point on, clubs and shows snowballed: more clubs meant more opportunities to

The hardy West Highland white terrier had its start in Scotland during the 1800s.

Life Cycle of the Domestic Dog

There are hundreds of domestic breeds available today, in sizes ranging from tiny (toy poodles weigh about 3 pounds) to enormous (Great Danes tip the scales at around 155). All of them develop at basically the same rate. Puppies are born in litters of one to over ten. Their eyes and ears remain closed for two to three weeks, although their sense of touch is acute. After the

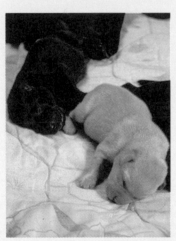

third week, their motor development begins, their eyes and ears open, and they start to walk.

At about two weeks, the pups' teeth begin to come in and the dam begins to wean them. She nurses the puppies for only a month, after which the breeder feeds them three meals a day from a bowl. The ideal time for pups to leave their litter is between the ages of eight and twelve weeks. The stage from three weeks to thirteen weeks is referred to as the socialization period, and it is extremely important in the development of a friendly

companion dog. Puppies at this stage must be in close contact with their mothers and with people if they are to become properly socialized. Experts point out that while the socialization period technically ends at thirteen weeks, in reality the process of socialization continues throughout a dog's life. Adult dogs who are deprived of human and animal contact for prolonged periods (for instance, in a kennel) will often revert to fearful, antisocial behavior.

After the socialization period, at about eighteen weeks, the pup enters her adolescence. Like human adolescence, this is a time of much turmoil and excitement as the dog learns how to behave in society. In many breeds, this period lasts until the dog is two years old, but in some it drags on until age three. This is the time when a dog should receive obedience training, although you can start your dog in puppy kindergarten as young as eight weeks. After about

three years of age, a dog's habits and temperament are fairly well established.

Life expectancy varies according to breed. Some small dogs such as fox terriers may live to be eighteen or twenty years old. Larger dogs such as boxers and German shepherds have a shorter life expectancy of about twelve years. A dog's longevity depends to a great extent on the quality of her life: if she gets plenty of exercise, is fed a nutritious diet, and is kept in a clean and loving environment, her chances of enjoying a long life are increased.

show dogs, while more shows further ignited the public's interest, leading more people to join the clubs. The first dog shows emphasized the great hunting dogs, but soon other breeds caught the public's fancy. Before long, the shows highlighted gundogs, sheepdogs, watchdogs, and companion dogs as well. Now, at the end of the twentieth century, approximately 10,000 competitive events are held each year under AKC rules in the U.S., and about 1,250,000 dogs are added to its registry annually.

There are about four hundred different breeds registered with dog clubs around the world. In North America, these breeds fall into seven categories: sporting dogs, hounds, working dogs, herding dogs, terriers, toys, and nonsporting dogs. Every breed has legions of admirers dedicated to preserving and improving it. More than any other time in history, we dote on dogs and rely on them to soothe our souls.

Dogs are still employed to hunt, herd our flocks, and guard our property. But their duties have expanded to other areas as well: dogs guide the sightless and assist the handicapped, sniff out narcotics for police and truffles for gourmets, rescue hikers, and cheer up hospitalized people. Above all, dogs offer us their loyalty, affection, and playful good nature.

Owning a dog is not like owning any other pet—a dog will demand your devotion and thrive on love and attention. In return, she'll brighten your life and perhaps expand your horizons. If you're unfamiliar with the streets in your neighborhood (or, for that matter, with your neighbors), walking your dog each day will change all that. A dog seeks connections—to you, your family, the other dogs on the block. She'll pull you along on her explorations, include you in her discoveries, and offer you unconditional friendship. Read on to learn everything you need to know to find the right dog and make sure she leads a happy, healthy life. With the great variety of breeds available today and the recent advances in veterinary science, there's never been a better time to own a dog.

Above: *Some dogs, such as this Great Pyrenees, work as therapy dogs.*

Below: *The pug is one of the oldest breeds of dog and is especially good with children.*

The Right Dog for You

2

The comradeship between people and dogs is unique in the natural world. With no other creature have we so closely shared work, friendship, and daily routines. A dog adds a certain spark to life—in fact, research has shown that when people come into contact with their dogs, their bodies instantly undergo physiological changes that put them in a state of well-being. Most dog lovers feel that life without a dog has a little too much "space" in it. They long for the particular warmth and cheer that a dog provides.

Yet the pressures of modern life make the decision to own a dog more complicated than it has been in the past. Long work hours, long commutes, and demanding schedules have changed the way we live, but the nature of the dog has remained the same. We can't expect a dog to adjust to our hectic lifestyles. Therefore, it is up to us as pet owners to make sure we can provide a home that is suited to a dog's needs.

Is Now the Right Time?

Owning a dog is usually a ten- to fifteen-year commitment, so it's unwise to buy one on impulse. Instead, carefully reflect on your situation now and in the foreseeable future. The two most important considerations are money and time.

The initial investment for a dog can be considerable, especially if you're buying a pedigreed animal.

Depending on the breed, a purebred dog bought from a reputable breeder can cost anywhere from $300 to $1500. Shelter dogs bought from humane societies and other rescue organizations typically cost $65 to $125.

In addition to the price of the dog, you'll need to purchase food, bedding, a collar and leash, bowls, toys, and a crate. Also, you'll probably enroll your puppy in obedience classes. Your puppy's first year will be a costly one, requiring regular checkups, vaccinations, and spaying or neutering. You may want to contact a veterinarian for an estimate on this essential care to find out if it's within your budget. After puppyhood, basic veterinary care is normally limited to a checkup and shots once a year, heartworm prevention in some parts of the country, occasional worming, and annual teeth cleaning for dogs over three years of age. If your dog becomes ill or has an accident, however, the bill can run into hundreds of dollars.

Grooming is not only healthy for the dog's skin and coat, but can be a pleasurable and bonding experience as well.

Grooming costs for most dogs are minimal unless you own a poodle, spaniel, or terrier, but flea products are another cost to consider. Shampoos, sprays, and the monthly flea prevention medications can be expensive. In some areas of the country, flea infestation is so widespread that professional house extermination is routine.

All in all, expect to spend several hundred dollars per year in addition to feeding costs to maintain your dog. If this figure sounds manageable, take some time to think over your other financial obligations for the next few years as well. Will you be purchasing a house with a sizable mortgage? Will you be starting a family? Will you be sending a child off to college? Any of these typical situations could change your financial picture

Having a dog means you're making a commitment to provide for that animal for the rest of his life, even if you have to move.

enough that there would no longer be room for a dog. This foresight is important; the unspoken promise you make to a puppy when you bring him home is that you will provide for his needs through all the years of his life.

Time is the other major factor affecting your decision to own a dog. Dogs require your attention, and that means more than simply feeding them and turning them into the yard to relieve themselves. A puppy needs training and supervision during his first year, and all dogs require exercise and the security of your affection and company. Dogs are pack animals, used to the companionship of others. For them, long hours spent in solitude are both lonely and stressful. Many behavior problems, such as excessive barking and destructive chewing, come from the boredom and anxiety of being left alone for ten or twelve hours a day while people are at work or in school.

Analyze your lifestyle honestly. Do you spend your day at the office, then rush to the gym or a meeting after dinner? Are your weekends full of activities that can't include a dog? Do you travel regularly, which would require that your dog be kenneled several times a month? Will you resent having to get up an hour earlier or go out again just after you've come home because the dog needs to be walked? All of these issues need to be weighed carefully with the dog's best interests in mind.

Again, look into the future to see how your plans may impact the time you have to spend with a dog. Will you be returning to school or getting a promotion that requires extra hours at the office? Will you be starting a family, and exhausting most of your time and energy caring for the baby? These important questions should never be brushed aside with the rationale that if all else fails, you can give the dog away. It is very difficult to place older dogs; many end their days at the local animal shelter.

For people who have demanding schedules but still want a dog, there are some creative solutions. The general rule of thumb is, if your dog must regularly spend more than six hours a day alone, you should provide him with access to the outdoors or companionship. Some people install a dog door to allow the dog to go in and out independently. (Make sure your yard is secure!) Others hire a dog walker or come home at noon for lunch. Sometimes a neighbor will walk the dog or bring him over to her house to visit with her dog. You may also want to consider having two dogs if it's economically feasible. Dogs do bond to each other and find comfort in each other's company. With a little planning, having a dog (or two) might work even if your schedule is relatively full.

Choosing the Right Breed

Most people choose a breed of dog by the way it looks. The beauty of the various breeds has enormous appeal, but bear in mind that each breed was developed for a specific purpose. Whether a dog is a sporting dog or a terrier or a toy breed will make a big difference in his needs for exercise, training, and

A dog door leading to a fenced-in yard is a great way to let Fido have access to the outdoors and get some exercise while you're away.

companionship. To decide which breed is the best match for you and your family, you'll need to understand how each breed's particular characteristics play out in a domestic setting.

For an overview of your choices, peruse an encyclopedia that gives detailed information on the history, purpose, character, and needs of all dog breeds. Although individuals within a breed will vary in temperament, most run fairly true to type because they've been selectively bred for thousands of years. (Mixed breed dogs usually carry the temperament of the breed they resemble the most.) As you familiarize yourself with the different breeds, you can begin to narrow down your choices to those that match your personal criteria for the ideal pet.

A basset hound is a good pet for people who like to snuggle at home.

How do you develop those criteria? It's a more subtle question than deciding between big and small, short hair or long. You'll need to carefully examine your lifestyle, your living situation, your age, the ages of your children, and the amount of time you wish to spend on activities such as grooming or training. You must also weigh each of these areas against the others. With over 140 breeds recognized by the AKC alone, there is sure to be a dog out there who is perfect for you.

Your activity level is a good place to start when deciding on a breed. Do you regularly spend time hiking and jogging? Or are you more sedentary, enjoying your free time curled up on the couch with a good book and a bowl of popcorn? Does a stroll around the neighborhood satisfy your need for the great outdoors? Think carefully about this. All dogs enjoy regular exercise, but some breeds will match your pace better than others. A person who loves the beauty of sporting dogs but is only moderately active would do better with a cocker spaniel than a weimaraner or an English setter, either of which will pester his owner tenaciously for the vigorous activity he needs every day. People who love to hike and run would do well with a Siberian husky or an Afghan hound, but these dogs may run off if unleashed; a more tractable dog such as a Labrador retriever or an Australian shepherd may be more practical. For sedentary types, a bulldog, basset hound, or shih tzu will be content to snuggle on the sofa for hours.

Size is often not the best indicator of activity level. Many people have made the mistake of getting Jack Russell terriers because they're small, only to discover that they need the same

More than meets the eye! Like other terriers, this rough-coated Jack Russell terrier is a high-energy dog who is happiest with constant attention and exercise.

amount of exercise as Border collies. Conversely, some of the large-boned, giant breeds are somewhat lethargic and slow moving. Mastiffs, for example, can be happy simply lying on a porch, majestically surveying their domain. If you buy a mastiff to accompany you jogging, you might be sorely disappointed.

Your age is another factor to consider when selecting a breed. Although many older people are quite active, there are other issues, such as handling and lifting, that might contribute to compatibility. An older person might find it easier to manage and train a cavalier King Charles spaniel than a rambunctious young golden retriever. A small- or medium-sized dog can be easier to bathe and groom, and less likely than a large dog to inadvertently knock people off their feet.

Whether or not there are children in the household (and their ages) is also critical to your choice of breeds. Most people feel that children and dogs go together, and they do, provided that you choose the right breed at the right time. Raising an infant and a puppy at the same time so that "they'll grow up together" may truly be impractical considering the demanding needs of both. Children, especially toddlers, need to be taught to handle dogs with kindness and to back off when a dog has "had enough." Small children may need to be separated from their pets when the play gets too rough. All children under the age of five should be supervised when playing with a dog.

Many people feel that small dogs are better with children because of their size, but this is usually not the case. Small dogs, especially toy breeds, are not suited for roughhousing; they sense their own fragility and can become nervous and snappish with youngsters. Larger, sturdier dogs are a much better choice. All of the retrievers are well known for their docility and tolerance for children and are popular with young, active families. Herding dogs are often wonderful choices, but sometimes the nipping at the heels that you'll see in Australian cattle dogs or Welsh corgis as they attempt to round everyone up can be irritating to younger children. Protection dogs such as rottweilers and bullmastiffs can be trustworthy with children, but they are a lot of dog and need the firm hand of an experienced adult.

Remember, even if you are purchasing a dog for your children, you will still be the person ultimately responsible for his care and training—children are not consistently reliable, no matter how good their intentions are.

The dog who suits your activity level, age, and the ages of your children must also fit in with the general atmosphere of your home. Are you a fastidious housekeeper or a person who is fairly relaxed about chores and clutter? Do you treasure a

Children need to be taught to treat animals with kindness and gentleness.

Opposite Top: Bred to retrieve, golden retrievers (and other dogs in the retriever family) are most content when they are carrying something in their mouths. If you've decided on a retriever, be sure you're willing to accept this behavior.

Opposite Bottom: The required time and costs for grooming should be a factor in choosing a breed that fits your lifestyle. A poodle's constantly growing curly coat requires much care.

Be aware of each breed's down sides. Sweet-natured Newfoundlands (Newfies) and other dogs with pendulous lips drool, a characteristic some tolerant dog lovers don't mind.

quiet atmosphere, or do you enjoy the buzz of a bustling household? Do you dress impeccably, or are you the jeans-and-sweatshirt type? More often than not, it is these seemingly minor details that make or break a person's relationship with a dog.

For fastidious housekeepers and natty dressers, dog hair is often a big issue. You may prefer a dog with a shorter coat, but you'll want to research coat type carefully, as it can be deceiving. Shorter-coated dogs such as German shepherds and dalmatians shed profusely. Some dogs, such as scent hounds, have short but oily coats that tend to have a strong odor. Without bathing your dog regularly, your house will take on these unpleasant smells.

Dogs with excessive facial wrinkling or pendulous lips such as shar-peis, bloodhounds, and Saint Bernards have enormously appealing expressions but engage in almost constant drooling and head shaking that will send long strings of saliva flying onto your clothes and furniture. (Carrying a cloth for

proactive wiping is a must.) Dogs with hairy faces such as Old English sheepdogs and some terriers have beards that are often odorous and unpleasantly wet after meals. If you will have a low tolerance level for these types of characteristics, choose another breed. The solution is not to banish Towser to the garage because he smells bad but to choose wisely in the beginning. A greyhound, poodle, or pug may be the right dog for you.

All dogs have characteristics that were bred into them for a purpose but may be at odds with your own temperament. Herding dogs and terriers can be annoying barkers. Huskies and malamutes enjoy a good howl. Retrievers have the habit of carrying around shoes and other personal items. Certain individual breeds, such as Samoyeds and Chesapeake Bay retrievers, are so affectionate and attention-seeking with their owners that they drive some people to distraction. Consult with a dog trainer about the quirks and the general trainability of each breed you're interested in, and any extra training that may be required.

Some breeds require a lot more grooming than others. This can be expensive if you have a poodle, or time-consuming if you have a collie or a Maltese. Some people find brushing their longhaired dog a relaxing way to spend quality time together; others find it a burdensome chore. Depending on the dog, you may need to include nail trimming, ear cleaning, tooth brushing, and eye cleaning in the regular grooming regimen.

Once you've selected the breeds that appeal to you the most, you can research them in greater depth by reading breed-specific books available in pet stores and libraries and by talking with reputable breeders. The breeders will tell you about the strengths and the drawbacks of the

Deciding on an Older Dog

For most people, getting a dog means buying a puppy. But you may want to consider adopting an older dog. There are a lot of advantages to bringing home a dog who is past the "terrible twos"—who won't chew up your furniture and is already housebroken.

Buying a mature animal eliminates the guesswork about temperament; after about three years of age, a dog's personality has stabilized. Adult dogs are calmer with children, and dogs who have already lived in a household with kids are used to their energy and unpredictability. The quieter disposition of an older dog (depending on the breed, of course) can also be a relief to some people. Older people, for example, may want the companionship of a dog without the intensity of those first two or three formative years.

Another bonus is that many mature dogs have already been through obedience training, which means not only are they housebroken, but they will quickly follow all the basic commands, making it easier for you to teach them the rules of your home. The possibility does exist that an adult dog will have some habits you don't like. Sometimes it is difficult, or even impossible, to retrain such a dog. It all depends on the dog, the behavior, and the owner.

Older dogs are always available at animal shelters, where you might be able to learn why the dog has been relinquished by his former owner. (Often the dog was simply inconvenient.) Few people are aware that beautiful purebred adults can also be purchased from reputable breeders. Typically these dogs have been returned to the breeder because they fell short in an area such as hunting or conformation, making them unsuitable for showing and breeding. Because good breeders promise to take back their dogs if an owner is dissatisfied, these "slightly imperfect" but lovely animals live with the breeder until they can find a new home. These dogs are often an excellent buy, as they have received the finest care and are usually well trained in obedience.

If you are a senior citizen, a parent with a lively family, or just a person who'd like the companionship of a dog without the hassle of puppyhood and adolescence, an older dog may be your best choice.

type of dog they breed, what that breed needs to thrive, and whether it is suitable for a novice or a more experienced owner. If a breeder tries to sell you a dog without giving you specific information or asking anything about your needs or situation, you'd best look elsewhere. This person is not interested in a good match that would guarantee the well-being of the dog, and chances are he or she is not selectively breeding for type and soundness of temperament.

Good Dog Citizenship

When you finally find the perfect dog for you, please practice good dog citizenship. Be aware of the leash laws and "poop scoop" requirements in your area. Ignoring them can lead to expensive fines, or worse yet, your dog getting hit by a car on a busy street.

License your dog in accordance with the local laws, and keep identification tags on him at all times. More permanent forms of identification are also available, such as tattoos and implanted microchips. It is a sad fact that only about 5 percent of unlicensed dogs picked up by animal control are ever reunited with their owners.

Also remember to be a good neighbor. Your neighbors do not want your dog defecating in their yards, turning over their garbage cans, or chasing their cats. No one wants to listen to your dog bark for hours on end while you're away. Contain your dog in a securely fenced yard or in your home when you are not out for a walk together. Train and socialize him to be a well-mannered pet, and if problem behaviors arise, get assistance from a qualified trainer. A dog who is not a nuisance for you is less likely to be a nuisance for your neighbors.

For millions of people around the world, owning a dog is a delightful and rewarding experience. It's worth taking the time to carefully research breeds before bringing a dog or puppy into your life. If you're aware of the nature of your chosen breed and the time and energy your dog will require of you, you're much more likely to forge a lasting, loving relationship with your dog.

For your dog's safety, always keep ID tags on your pet, and use a leash when going for walks.

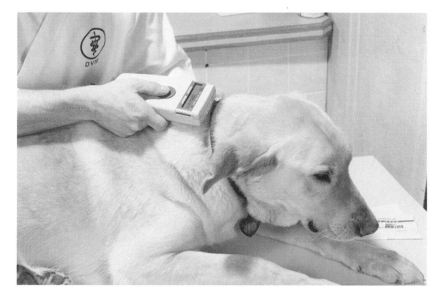

With the help of scanners (left), a tiny microchip smaller than a stamp (above) implanted under a dog's skin can help people find out where the dog lives.

Choosing a Puppy

3

After hours of soul-searching, poring over dog books, and hashing out the pros and cons of different breeds, many people shopping for a puppy leap right in and buy the first cute one they see. She may be staring wistfully through a pet store window or frolicking with her brothers and sisters in a cardboard box outside the supermarket. Those brown eyes melt into you, and you can't resist . . .

Don't give in to temptation! Although an unknown, unresearched dog may turn out to be a fine family pet, it isn't worth the risk. You could end up with an ill-tempered or chronically ill dog who will try your patience, tax your wallet, and possibly wreak havoc on your family life. Not to be overlooked is the welfare of the dog, who deserves an owner who understands

her needs and is willing to meet them. If you have children, be sure to include them in the selection process. And take time to find just the right puppy for you; it will pay off in years of companionship and mutual affection.

Where Should You Buy Your Puppy?

You have four places to go to purchase a dog: a pet store, a humane shelter, a hobby breeder, and a backyard breeder. It's possible to find a delightful pet at any of these, but some sources are more reliable than others.

Many people buy dogs on impulse, which is why so many dog owners purchase their puppies at pet stores. For a while, pet stores were viewed suspiciously by the public due to a rash of news stories about puppy mills—unscrupulous breeders who raise puppies in deplorable conditions, then ship them off to pet stores around the country. These puppies often are ill or bear genetically undesirable traits.

As a result of all the bad publicity, most pet stores now offer to replace any puppy who is found to have a serious disorder or defect. Most stores swear that they never buy from puppy mills. (The potential dog owner usually has to take their word for it.) The pet industry has a voluntary organization of commercial breeders, the American Professional Pet Distributors, Inc., that sets standards for its members and is committed to improving the image of the industry.

People who own or work at pet stores usually do so because

People have come to this pet store hoping to find just the right dog for them to take home.

they love animals; they genuinely want to provide you with a healthy pet. Even so, because of the nature of the industry, breeding standards at pet stores cannot be as stringent as those followed by hobby breeders. Pet stores have to sell a certain number of pets to stay in business, so they usually aren't as picky as hobby breeders when it comes to genetic screening, keeping records on litter mates or lineage, or testing the overall health of the dog. For these reasons, if you are a novice dog owner and intend to enter your dog in shows it's not recommended that you buy a puppy from a pet store.

Whether you're a novice or veteran dog owner, the humane shelter can be a wonderful source for a dog, particularly an older one. There is an enormous canine overpopulation problem today, and shelters are overflowing with loving, sometimes even trained animals whose owners could no longer care for them.

Most shelters accept both stray dogs and those who are dropped off by their owners. As you walk down the rows of cages, your heartstrings are sure to be tugged at the sight of so many abandoned animals. Usually, each dog's cage has a card on it explaining why the dog was left at the shelter. Sometimes the card lists behavioral problems such as barking or digging, but quite often the pet just became inconvenient—perhaps the owner moved out of town or to a residence that wouldn't permit animals. Many purebred dogs, especially popular breeds such as Labrador retrievers, can be found at shelters. Puppies are available as well.

When you adopt a dog at a shelter, you can never be sure about her background because owners who drop off their animals are sometimes reluctant to admit their true motives. (With strays, of course, there is no way of knowing about background.) Therefore, you run some risk of getting a pet with behavioral problems you hadn't bargained for. It's especially difficult to tell if your dog will be a barker, because most dogs bark a lot when they are in a shelter.

That said, bear in mind that thousands of people each year adopt pets from humane shelters and are delighted with them.

Many dogs at humane shelters have been abandoned and are waiting for someone to take them home.

Potential owners are given ample time to play with animals at the shelter before making their choices to be sure they "click" with their new pets.

What about the health of shelter animals? Again, it's somewhat of a wild card, but the adoption fee (typically between $65 and $125) usually includes a medical checkup, all the basic shots, and the partial cost of spaying or neutering—a bargain considering most veterinarians' rates. If you are not planning to breed or show your dog and are open to many different breeds, consider getting your dog at a shelter.

A reputable hobby breeder, such as this breeder of pugs, is concerned with the welfare of each puppy and exhibits passion for perfecting the breed.

If you do want a show dog, there's only one good choice: a reputable hobby breeder. Hobby breeders devote years to the study and improvement of a breed. They're not breeding dogs for the money. In fact, they are called hobby breeders because, unlike commercial breeders who provide puppies for retail pet stores, they usually have another means of livelihood besides selling litters. This breeder's "hobby" could more accurately be called a passion, and his or her dedication will translate into a healthier, better adjusted pet for you.

The backyard breeder, another outlet for buying a dog, is a source of much controversy among dog lovers. These breeders are usually people who own a dog and decide to breed her, sometimes for dubious reasons. Maybe they want to show

Ask the Breeder

There are some specific questions you should ask breeders before purchasing a dog:

- How long have they been breeding this breed?

- Do they have other breeds?

- Do they belong to a local or national dog club?

- How many litters have their dogs had?

- What is the breed's life span?

- Is this breed easy to train and housebreak?

- What are the most significant physical problems within the breed?

- Are there any temperament problems or behavioral difficulties to be expected?

- What kind of contract, conditions, or guarantees are involved in the sale of a puppy?

their children "the miracle of birth" as the puppies are born, or perhaps they believe they can make a few dollars each year by selling a litter or two. The backyard breeder generally is not very knowledgeable about the breed. And quite often, the breeder will mate a dam with any convenient sire of the same breed, with little regard to genetics, bloodlines, or breed improvement.

Puppies raised by backyard breeders can turn out to be loving, well-socialized family pets. But if you are going to get your pet from a breeder and go to all the trouble of researching breeders and speaking with several of them, why choose a backyard breeder over a more dedicated hobby breeder? Most people don't intend to make this mistake, and although there are some marked differences, some people can't tell the two apart. After all, hobby breeders frequently breed their dogs in their backyards. How, then, do you find a legitimate, well-qualified breeder?

Finding the Best Dog Breeders

A good place to begin looking for a breeder is the AKC's information line: (900) AKC-PUPS. They'll send you a list of breeders who have been recommended by the parent club, the national club of the specific breed. If you want a breed that's not registered with the AKC, you'll need to contact other local or national clubs, registries, or individual dog owners for breeder recommendations. The classified sections of dog magazines and local veterinarians may prove helpful here. While you're talking with the vet, ask a few questions about the breed you are considering. Are there any health or temperament problems associated with the breed? Any quirks? Has the vet heard mostly glowing reports about the breed, or are owners reporting problems? If so, what are they?

A good hobby breeder answers all your questions freely and probably has questions to ask you, too. Be prepared to sign contracts and receive paperwork and certificates.

If you've done your homework and researched your breed, you'll have a solid base of knowledge about your potential pet when you meet with breeders. As you're quizzing them about the specifics of their litters, you'll want to assess their philosophies and approaches to breeding. This is one area where the difference between backyard breeders and hobby breeders becomes apparent.

Reputable hobby breeders will be forthright about answering all of your questions; in fact, they love to talk about their dogs. After a few minutes of conversation, it will probably become clear that their primary goal in breeding is to improve the breed, not to profit from the pups. They nearly always belong to a local or national dog club. It's best to choose someone who has been breeding for at least five years, so that you can benefit from his or her experience with the breed if you run into difficulties later. Most breeders, but not all, focus their passion on a single breed.

Tests and Paperwork

Your breeder should supply you with a health guarantee package attesting to the good health of your puppy. The health guarantee package should include:

🐕 Clearance certificates stating that both parents of your puppy are free of ailments or genetic problems common to the breed. When you're researching your breed, read about the typical ailments and make sure that all appropriate clearance certifications on the parents are included in your package. In addition, there should be a clause assuring that the breeder will replace the puppy or return your money should any congenital defect become apparent within a specified time period after purchase.

🐕 Certificates from the vet stating that your pet has been wormed, vaccinated, and given a general checkup

🐕 A clause requiring you to take the puppy to a vet within two or three days of purchase to confirm that she's in good health

Additional paperwork involved in purchasing a puppy includes:

🐕 A bill of sale stating the puppy's price

🐕 Permanent registration papers or a registration application

🐕 A four- or five-generation pedigree listing the puppy's ancestors, including their genetic screening certification numbers

It's essential that you receive all of these documents; if your breeder balks at providing them, do not proceed with the purchase.

A good breeder will be honest about the breed's drawbacks—and every breed has some. Those breeders who insist that their breed is flawless are suffering from what is called kennel blindness. Why should this matter to you? Because when you need to call on the breeder for help, he or she may fail to agree that you need assistance; after all, they've never had a problem with their dogs.

A breeder may question you about the type of home you can provide a puppy and if you have any other pets. How willing are you to forgive occasional mishaps?

If you've done a good job of researching your chosen breed, your questions can be especially revealing. First, you'll get a sense of the breeder's knowledge, indicating whether the person is a backyard or a hobby breeder. Second, you'll be able to root out the kennel-blind breeder by comparing his or her answers to the facts you've learned. And third, hopefully you'll pick up some additional helpful information about the pros and cons of the breed.

What a Breeder Looks for in an Owner

Dedicated breeders have an abiding concern for their dogs. When you're finished asking your questions, be prepared to answer a few yourself. Any good breeder will quiz you to make sure the pups are going to a good home. Most breeders are especially concerned that you have an understanding of the breed and what it will take to properly care for the dog. If you have a family, the breeder will likely emphasize that an adult—not the kids—will probably end up doing most of the pet-related chores.

The breeder will want to be reassured that your lifestyle is well suited for the breed's temperament. He or she may ask you to take time off from work or promise to come home during your lunch hour during the first few weeks if no one else will be home to care for the puppy. The breeder will also look for signs that you are patient and willing to forgive the puppy for inevitable slipups during the first months (or years!).

Most breeders will ask you about the environment in which you'll be keeping the dog—they'll want to know that your yard is safely fenced and that you will have a crate and/or a special area prepared for your puppy in your home. If you live in an apartment, the breeder may ask you where and how often you'll exercise the dog.

Finally, breeders trust prospective owners who are eager to learn everything about the pup. They know that owning a dog is a continual learning experience, and if you are anxious to close the deal and seem uninterested in gleaning every bit of information you can at the first meeting, a breeder may (rightfully) doubt your commitment to the dog.

Picking a Pup from the Litter

Once you are satisfied that your breeder is reliable and honest, you'll finally get to the heart of the matter—choosing a dog from a litter of irresistible puppies. Before you let yourself get swept away, you'll need to assess the puppy's physical condition and temperament. All of the following guidelines apply to adult dogs as well as puppies.

If your breeder has provided you with the necessary health guarantee package and you're well versed in the desirable physical traits of your breed, you stand a good chance of being able to pick the prime pup in a litter. A brief on-the-spot examination will confirm that your puppy is a healthy one.

First look at the dog's head and features. Pale gums and tongue may be signs of anemia or intestinal parasites. Overlapping front teeth indicate incorrect bite or malocclusion. A hacking cough may indicate parasites or a respiratory infection. Discharge in the pup's eyes may mean she has worms or a chronic eye ailment. Don't forget to examine the ears: ear canals dirty with wax and debris indicate ear mites, while crusty ear tips suggest sarcoptic mange.

Before buying a puppy, look her over carefully to be sure she is healthy.

Then check out the rest of the pup's body. Her coat should look healthy and clean. A dirty coat, inflamed skin, or hair loss could be signs of fleas, mange, or ringworm. The pup who limps or has a faltering gait may already be showing signs of hip dysplasia or bone or joint disease. Inflammation around the pup's anus indicates diarrhea or a digestive disorder. In a female, vaginal discharge or pasting of hair around the vagina are signs of vaginitis. In a male, both testicles should be present in the scrotum. A bulging navel indicates an umbilical hernia; although it sounds serious, in a puppy this condition is easily repaired and may even disappear on its own. If your pup

This English bulldog puppy has an umbilical hernia, which isn't serious and even may go away on its own.

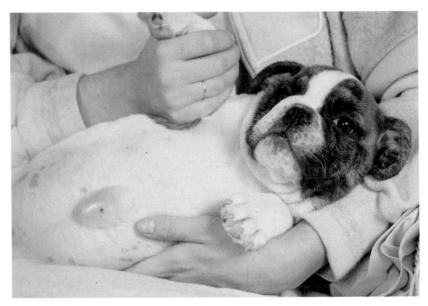

passes this brief exam, you're ready for the fun part—sizing up her personality.

The ideal time to purchase a pup is when she is eight to twelve weeks old. By then she will have established a pattern of primary socialization, meaning that she will have learned how to get along with people and other dogs. This is a crucial period in a pup's development, which is why it is unwise to remove a puppy from the litter before eight weeks of age.

You can get the first inkling of your puppy's temperament by observing the way her mother behaves and interacts with people. The dam might be cautious around you at first, which is natural, but soon she should warm up and allow you to approach her and scratch her back and ears. If the sire is also on hand, observe him as well, looking for signs that he is neither too aggressive nor too shy.

Look for a balance between dominance and submission in

your pup. Seek out a puppy who is active, alert, and playful, and then put her through the series of simple tests described below. None of these tests are foolproof, but they do provide a basis for assessing a pup's personality and temperament.

If you get your puppy from a breeder, see if you can spend some time with the mother. If she's fun to be with, her pups, too, are likely to have good temperaments.

Bear in mind that puppies have bad days, too. If you're uncertain about a puppy after running through the tests, yet you're still strongly drawn to her, come back another day and try again. The criteria below are geared for an animal who would be suitable for first-time dog owners and families with small children. Experienced owners and older kids will be better able to cope with dominant dogs, while a senior citizen or quiet adult might do well with a shy or slightly submissive pet.

1. Friendliness: Place the puppy on the ground in an area somewhat removed from the rest of the litter. Walk a few feet away, squat down, and call the puppy to you in a cheerful voice, patting the ground in front of you. If the pup runs right to you and perhaps bites or mouths your hands, she may tend to be aggressive. If the pup doesn't come at all, is extremely hesitant, or crawls to you, she may be overly shy or antisocial. A well-adjusted pup will come quickly with her tail level or

Take the time to test the puppy's willingness to follow. How she reacts may tell you if she has tendencies to be a dominant or submissive dog.

How a puppy responds to a piece of crumpled-up paper will give you a clue about the pup's temperament.

slightly down. She may try to crawl into your lap, but she won't attempt to bite.

2. Following: Stand up and walk away from the puppy without encouraging her to follow you. If the puppy follows you closely and perhaps nips at your feet, she's dominant; if she doesn't follow, follows slowly, or crawls, she's shy. The pup who follows hesitantly is best suited for family life.

3. Retrieving: Crumple up a piece of paper, show it to the puppy, then toss it a few feet in front of her. The dominant pup will chase the paper and either bring it back or attempt to play keepaway with you. The shy pup will either ignore the paper or move off in another direction entirely. A well-balanced pup will chase after the paper, perhaps hesitantly, and bring it at least part way back.

4. Trainability: Stand and hold the paper over the pup's head, crumpling it noisily as you slowly move the paper toward the puppy's tail. Tell the pup to sit, and when she does, praise her enthusiastically and let her play with the paper for a few moments. Repeat four or five times. A dominant pup will jump on you

for the paper, while the shy pup will sit and then lie down, or simply walk away. A well-balanced puppy may jump up a few times but will sit down by the third or fourth try.

5. Social Handling: This tests the pup's tolerance for being touched—especially important in a family with small children. Touch the puppy all over on her head, shoulders, back, ears, muzzle, and paws. If she growls at you, jumps, or nips at your hands, she is dominant. If she rolls over and bares her belly or walks away, she's submissive. A pup who responds by wiggling and licking your hands is your best bet.

The pup who is a real live wire may not be the best choice for a family pet. It's natural to conclude that your high-energy kids should be matched with a high-energy dog, but those pups can sometimes develop into overly aggressive animals. Although these tests are not etched in stone, do pay attention to the results when you are making your final decision. From the moment you accept that puppy into your life and heart, she will be depending on you to understand her nature and provide her with a loving, stable home.

After going through puppy personality tests, this yellow Labrador retriever puppy has found a family who's just right for her!

Preparing for Your New Dog

4

When expectant mothers get the urge to nest—to prepare their homes for a new baby—they go over every room with a fine-tooth comb and spend hours shopping for a crib and blankets, baby clothes, and toys. You'll need to go through a similar process before bringing home your new dog, especially if he's a puppy. Older dogs often have been house-trained already, so most of the advice in this chapter applies to puppies. Still, some of the basic necessities for puppies will be needed by older dogs as well.

Setting Up a Home for Your Dog

You'll want your home to be warm and welcoming for your new pet, but from the very beginning you must be prepared to set some limits. If you don't, your inquisitive and energetic puppy can quickly destroy your property or even endanger himself.

Dogs, like people, need a comfortable place to sleep and eat—their own private territory. Likewise, you and your family need an area in which to confine the pup so you can keep an eye on him. Before bringing home your new dog, clear an area to be his home base. A corner of the kitchen, the laundry room, or a screened-in porch are good choices; these spots see plenty of activity during the day and seclusion and quiet at night. A bathroom might also work if it's not too removed from the area where the family spends most of its time.

Watch Out for These Puppy Habits

Chewing: Furniture, rugs, and electric cords are all targets. Children's toys are especially appealing to puppies.

Digging: Pups like to dig anywhere they can; they'll unearth plants and try to tunnel under gates and fences.

Clawing: Screens, gates, and doors intended to restrain puppies are all susceptible to damage.

Shredding: A pup can turn books, magazines, and newspapers into confetti in short order.

Exploring: Anything that can be tipped over—especially trash cans—is fair game for an inquisitive pup.

Don't exile your new pet to the backyard or to the basement, where it is cold, dark, and closed off from family activities. Your dog, after all, should be part of your household. Banishing such a social animal as a dog, especially for the first few nights, is cruel. Frightened or lonely, he's liable to whine, bark, and howl tenaciously, ensuring that you'll have sleepless nights, too.

You'll probably need to purchase a baby gate to cordon off your dog's special area. Many kitchens have open floor plans, making these gates a necessity to keep a dog out of trouble. But even if you confine your dog to a room that has a door, such as a laundry room, you don't want him to be entirely shut off from the family. Baby gates can be purchased at some large pet stores, baby stores, or children's stores such as Toys "R" Us. They also turn up frequently at yard sales. Puppies are a lot more determined and wily than infants, and for that reason, wood-and-mesh gates are not a good choice: a pup can use the mesh as a toehold and scramble up over the top. Your best bets are plastic or wooden gates that mount to the wall with screws or use a strong pressure-mounting system.

Choosing a Dog Crate

Dog crates are invaluable tools for training your puppy and make an ideal home base for your dog. The crate serves as a place to sleep, nap, and retreat to when family activities are too frenetic. A crate is also a practical way to transport your dog to and from the vet or on family outings.

You have two styles of crates to choose from: molded plastic or fiberglass, and wire. Molded crates, which can be dismantled easily for cleaning or traveling, are durable and are made of three parts: top, bottom, and door. Because they are enclosed, molded crates provide a lot of privacy and are especially suited to puppies who crave a cozy den. Wire crates, on the other hand, are open and offer good ventilation and viewing but little privacy. A towel or blanket draped over the outside of the crate can alleviate this problem.

Your dog's crate needs to be large enough to comfortably accommodate him when he is full grown. Think of the crate as a snug retreat for your pet—he'll need enough room to turn around (at his full adult height), but not much more. If your dog has too much space, he may be tempted to sleep in one corner of the crate and defecate in another, undermining your efforts at house-training.

Dog Proofing Your House

Dogs are curious creatures, so don't be surprised if one day you come home to a trail of litter, chewed socks, and shredded books. Like toddlers, dogs seek out avenues of escape, and once free, will explore every nook and cranny of your home, and what they find may be harmful. If you've never owned dogs before, you may be surprised at the extent of damage

Puppies can get into a lot of irresistibly fun trouble; it's up to you to dog proof your home and keep Puppy—and your valuables—safe.

Why puppy proof? Plants and flowers and other fascinating objects can be tempting to a dog who is getting to know the sights, smells, and sounds of a world new to him. Plan ahead and think like a pup: remove breakable items that could fall prey to your puppy's curiosity or clumsiness.

they can do if they have access to vulnerable areas. Don't let this dampen your enthusiasm. Remember, puppies grow up, get trained, and become civilized members of the household before you know it! The antics that may exasperate you during the first few months will provide plenty of humorous anecdotes later on.

To protect your new dog from harm, and to safeguard your belongings, you'll need to dog proof your house.

Inside the house, inspect every room for likely hazards. Clear away glassware, pottery, baskets, books, magazines, and precious linens and heirlooms that could be destroyed. Put houseplants out of reach; potting soil stirs a dog's digging instincts. Some houseplants are toxic if ingested and should be removed altogether. Your veterinarian or local nursery can provide you with a list of dangerous species.

Make sure all cabinet doors are secured with childproof latches, especially those cabinets in which you store cleaning items, chemicals, medicines, and packaged foods—dogs and puppies can chew through plastic. Not only can dogs get sick if they consume the contents, they can choke on the plastic.

Be as vigilant with your new dog as you would be with a baby. Put away small items such as needles, pens, candles, coins, and buttons that could be swallowed. Don't leave candy or cigarettes out. Hide electrical cords or secure them to the baseboards and cover trash cans, preferably with a latched lid.

One way to discourage your pup from chewing on items that can't be hidden away is to coat them with a vile-tasting substance. You can buy a commercial product such as Bitter Apple (the cream version is best for furniture) or use Tabasco sauce. You can also make your own cream by mixing cayenne pepper with petroleum jelly. To protect your draperies, buy masking tape that has adhesive on both sides, sprinkle cayenne pepper on one side, and stick the other side to the hem of the drapes.

Dog proofing your home will probably mean a change in family habits. Teach youngsters that toys left out will likely be chewed to bits, not to mention put the pup at risk. Even non-toxic crayons and clay can be harmful to your dog if ingested in large quantities.

Get into the habit of closing closet doors, unscreened windows, and toilet lids. You don't want to encourage your pet

Even flowers such as tulips can be dangerous. Keep poisonous plants safely out of Puppy's reach, or better yet, out of the house.

to drink out of the toilet. Toilet bowl cleaners are alkaline and will make your dog sick. Until your pup and family are well trained, be safe and don't use toilet cleaners. It's helpful to post signs near closets, toilets, and toy boxes to remind family members to follow the new rules.

If your dog will have access to a garage or workroom, make sure chemicals and tools are locked away there as well. When working on projects and using power tools, keep your curious dog or pup out of the area. Be diligent about cleaning up after each project. Sweep up nails, wood, scraps, and other debris. Clean up spills, especially antifreeze. Antifreeze is deadly if swallowed, and its sweet odor attracts dogs. For cleanup, use cat litter to absorb the liquid, then sweep it up and discard it in a secure trash can. Don't simply hose down antifreeze and oil spills; water will not remove the toxicity.

Inspect your yard for hazards as well. Pick up anything your dog is likely to chew or ingest—most any object is fair game. Coil hoses and store on a hose cart, put tools and toys away, and take cushions off the patio furniture if you don't want them soiled or chewed.

If you plan to leave your dog outdoors unattended, make sure you have a solid, secure fence. Walk the perimeter of your yard looking for holes where a small pup might squeeze through. Fill these holes with gravel, rocks, or chicken wire to discourage the dog from staging an escape. Repair any loose boards in wooden fences, and make sure your dog won't be able to dig beneath the fence.

Pools and hot tubs can be dangerous if they're not properly covered or secured. If your dog jumps into a pool or hot tub and can't find his way out, he may become agitated and could then easily drown. To prevent this, your best bet is to fence off the pool or hot tub from the rest of the yard. This will protect your dog even if someone forgets to cover the pool.

Pesticides can be another danger to your dog. If your dog is going to spend a good deal of time outdoors, use only non-toxic pesticides that contain pyrethrin. Talk to your local nursery about natural ways to remove garden pests. To keep your pup out of your prize tomatoes or roses, put a fence around your garden. If you find it impractical or undesirable to fence in your garden, consider putting the fence around the dog instead by building a dog run.

Dog proofing extends to the yard as well. Fence in your garden if you don't want your puppy romping in it.

This golden retriever puppy finds green plants tasty. To satisfy this urge, plant a garden of safe plants and herbs for your pup's chewing pleasure and health.

Safe and Poisonous Plants

Landscaping and gardens may pose a problem. There are many plants and trees that are poisonous to dogs. Here is a partial listing:

Nontoxic Plants	Mildly Toxic Plants	Very Toxic Plants
SAFE	**MILDLY POISONOUS**	**DANGEROUS**
Baby's Breath	Aloe Vera	Azalea
Begonia	Avocado (seeds,	Caladium
Dandelion	leaves, stem)	Elderberry
Fuchsia	Chrysanthemum	English Ivy
Gardenia	Fern	English Yew
Hibiscus	Honeysuckle	Foxglove
Jade Plant	Iris	Holly
Lilac	Pansy	Hydrangea
Rubber Plant	Poinsettia	Larkspur
Snap Dragon	Potato (all green parts)	Lily of the Valley
Spider Plant	Tomato (all green parts)	Mistletoe (greenleaf)
Yucca	Tulip	Morning Glory
Zinnia	Weeping Willow	Oleander
		Primrose
		Wisteria
		Yellow Jasmine

For a complete list of toxic plants in your area, check with a veterinarian, nursery, or poison control center.

Buying the Basics for Your Dog

The novice pet owner will need to stock his or her home with basic canine provisions. Most people choose to buy a crate for their dog, but a baby gate is another choice. Old towels will be needed to clean up spills or to use as padding inside the crate. You can also get a dog bed or basket that fits inside the crate, but many small puppies do just as well nestled on an old towel. You'll want to have the proper cleansers for accidents—Nature's Miracle and other similar cleansers get rid of offensive odors. Don't use ammonia-based disinfectants, as they may remind your pup of the smell of his own urine and prompt him to soil the same area again.

You'll need two dishes—one for water and one for food. Heavy plastic, ceramic, and stainless steel bowls are all suitable. If possible, the bases should be rimmed with rubber so

Dog Proofing

Check off items on this list to help you make sure you have dog proofed your house and yard. Taking these preventive measures will save you frustration and protect your dog from accidents.

Kitchen and Laundry

- All cabinets have been secured with childproof locks
- Trash cans have locked lids or are kept in an inaccessible cabinet
- Food is inaccessible
- Plastic bags are inaccessible
- Appliance cords are secured
- All cleaning and laundry soaps are locked away

Living Areas

- Breakables are out of reach
- Plants are out of reach
- Cords are hidden or secured to baseboards
- Small items are cleared from table tops
- Books and magazines are inaccessible
- Heirlooms or precious furniture (chairs, small tables) have been removed
- Baskets, sewing, and toys are stored
- Bathroom cabinets have been secured with childproof locks
- Shampoos, lotions, soaps are out of reach

Garage and Workroom

- Tools and chemicals are stored in lockers or storage boxes
- Garden tools are stored away
- Trash can lids are secure

Yard

- Fence is secure
- Potted plants have been moved out of reach
- Toys are stored away
- Garden is inaccessible
- Lawn cushions have been removed
- Garden hose is coiled and secured on a roller

they don't slide. If your dog is going to spend any time locked outdoors, buy a second water bowl to keep in the yard. Of course, you'll need dog food made especially for your dog's age group.

Your dog will also need a snap or buckle-type collar (choke collars should be used only for training; they can be dangerous for your dog, particularly in the hands of a child), identification tags, and a leash. Retractable leashes allow your dog more freedom of movement while still under your control. You'll also need a grooming kit specific to your breed. It should include a brush, comb, nail clippers, and brush for cleaning teeth.

And don't forget about toys. Chew toys are a necessity, especially since dogs go through an intense teething period from about four or five months until about six or seven months. Younger puppies, too, love and need to chew. Don't buy a chew toy that is harder than the puppy's teeth or that has small parts such as squeakers on which he could choke.

It seems like a lot of baggage for one small pup. Bear in mind, however, that most of these purchases will be with your dog throughout his lifetime. And now that your house is dog proofed and your crate is ready and waiting, let's bring that puppy home!

A well-ventilated crate, along with food, bowls, toys, a leash, and grooming products, should get you and your new family member off to a great start.

Bringing Your Dog Home

5

You've spent weeks, maybe months, looking for the right breed. You've prepared your home, purchased the necessities, and now the long-awaited day has arrived—you're ready to bring your new dog home. These first few weeks together will be a special time for you and your pet, as you build the trust and love that are the cornerstones of a rewarding relationship. You'll have plenty of delightful moments, but be prepared for some frustrating times as well. Remember, your dog or puppy will need a lot of attention and patience as she gets used to her new family and learns the rules of the house.

Introducing Your Dog to Her New Home

Dogs and puppies need to explore their new surroundings to satisfy their curiosity and calm their fears. You can allow adult dogs to explore the entire house and yard, but confine puppies to a small area. It's important to stay with your dog while she explores to prevent any mishaps. If you take the dog outside, make sure she is on a leash or in a secure area so she can't bolt if she gets frightened.

During this get-acquainted period, the family should be calm and attentive. Spend a lot of time playing with your dog and keep the house as quiet as possible. Loud noises and boisterous children can frighten a new pup and make an adult dog nervous.

When dogs and pups feel anxious, they seek out a private place—under a chair, behind the sofa, or in a snug, quiet corner—so introduce your dog to her crate right away, and give her plenty of time to sniff and explore. An old towel or a dog bed or basket will make the crate more appealing.

How do you entice your pup into her crate? It takes some time and a few proven techniques. A bribe is a good place to begin. Prop the door to the crate open and put a treat inside. Let the dog grab the treat. Most likely she'll dart back out immediately, but that's to be expected. Put another treat inside, and repeat the process several times—you want your dog to associate the crate with something good such as a treat. Then put the dog's water bowl and empty food bowl inside the crate. At mealtime, add food to the dish and leave it inside the crate, still keeping the door open. Leave another treat and some toys inside. Slowly your dog will begin to feel comfortable in the crate.

After a few days, begin to feed your dog in the crate with the door shut. Keep the door shut for a half hour or so the first day. Every day, increase the time. If your dog whines or cries, let her know you are near, but don't let her out immediately.

Even adult dogs need some quiet playtime and reassurance on the first day in their new home.

By using a treat and some patience, you can encourage your new puppy to enter a crate while earning her trust.

Your goal is to get your dog to associate the crate with comfort—food, sleep, and privacy. Create a positive environment by making sure the crate is always clean. Wipe up food and water spills as soon as you see them, keep the bedding free of dirt and fleas, and scrub up any accidents using Nature's Miracle or another odor-removing cleanser. Keeping your dog's favorite toys in the crate will encourage her to spend time there.

The crate should be a retreat for your dog, so respect her privacy—don't let children play in or around the crate, and don't drag your dog out of it against her will. Don't lock your dog in the crate for long periods of time or use the crate as a disciplinary device. If you do, she will associate the crate with punishment instead of comfort.

You can lessen your puppy's loneliness during the first few nights in her new home by providing such comforts as a ticking clock, a hot-water bottle, and a stuffed animal. Remember to leave papers nearby!

Separation Blues—How to Avoid Sleepless Nights

The first few nights in her new home will be difficult for your dog and most likely for you as well. Puppies separated from their litter will feel confused and lonely, and adult dogs might feel vulnerable and excited, making it difficult for them to settle down and sleep. Prepare for this inevitability and be patient.

Puppies are used to the security and protection a litter provides; it's the denning instinct that dogs have inherited from their wolf ancestors. Puppies who are accustomed to their mother's warmth will whine or yelp, a natural response to being separated from the litter.

To make these first nights more comfortable for you and your pup, set up a bedtime routine and follow it each evening. First, make sure your puppy has eaten dinner. Next, spend some time playing with your puppy. The more tuckered out your pup gets, the better she'll sleep. Right before you put her in the crate, give her an opportunity to relieve herself.

For comfort, place a small clock in the puppy's bedding. The

Adult dogs as well as puppies need to be exercised before bedtime.

ticking of the clock, a reminder of mother's heartbeat, will soothe her. A hot-water bottle tucked inside a blanket will provide more comfort and warmth. Make sure your pup has food, water, and toys nearby, and spread newspapers outside the crate so she can relieve herself during the night. Keep the door to the crate open so your pup can get to her papers.

If your puppy whines while she's in her crate at night, speak to her soothingly for a few minutes, then quietly move away. Try to leave her alone until she falls asleep, even if you hear an occasional whimper. If the crate is a wire one, you might try putting a towel over it to make it darker and provide more of a sense of enclosure and protection.

Some new owners may want to put the puppy's crate in the bedroom, so the puppy can be nearby if she begins to whine. This makes it easy for you to reach down and pet her and gives the puppy a sense of security. One word of caution, however. If you put your puppy's bed next to your own, and you don't plan on having her sleep in your bedroom her whole life, make sure to move the crate out of the bedroom within two or three days. If you wait any longer, your pup may resist being moved to a separate room.

An adult dog will usually get used to her home faster than a puppy will. Bedtime should not be much of a problem, either. But just in case, try to make time to thoroughly exercise your new dog before bed. A quick run in the backyard or a game of fetch will help her get a good night's rest.

As with puppies, make sure your dog has food, water, and toys nearby. Take her out before bedtime and let her relieve herself. If your dog is going to sleep in a crate, prop open the crate door and use a baby gate to prevent her from wandering through the house during the night. If your dog is going to sleep outside, be attentive if she whines or howls—not only for the dog's sake but for your neighbors' as well.

Housebreaking Your Dog

Dogs are instinctively clean animals who don't like to soil their sleeping area. For that reason, it's fairly easy to paper-train even young puppies (eight weeks and older). When it comes to housebreaking dogs, consistency, flexibility, patience, and plenty of affectionate praise are required. Dogs need consistent instruction—a predictable pattern of behavior they can respond to. Canines can't learn a new behavior immediately, no matter how insistent you are, so patience is essential. And because dogs can't interpret our needs and we can't always interpret theirs, you'll need to be flexible and adapt your training to your dog's preferences and temperament.

Most puppies can be paper-trained when they are eight to twelve weeks old. But they do not physiologically develop full control of their bowels or bladder until about the twelfth week. Keep this in mind when mishaps occur. Despite their lack of control, puppies will certainly give you cues when it's time: they may begin sniffing for a spot or may display a general anxiousness. It's your job to interpret these signs.

Paper training should take place in a confined area outside of—but near—your puppy's crate. Be understanding of mishaps while training and make your new pup feel safe.

Paper-training works best in a confined area, such as a laundry room, spare room, or kitchen, that has an easy-to-clean floor. This should also be the area where your pup eats and sleeps. As you know, puppies rarely soil their sleeping area, so if you use a crate, place papers outside the crate. The crate will most likely be too large for your puppy at first, so fill the extra space with a box turned upside down to prevent the puppy from using this area to relieve herself.

Place papers over most of the floor area. During the first few days, whenever the puppy shows signs of needing to relieve herself, carry her to the paper-covered area. Take care not to startle your pup by whisking her away too quickly. This will only confuse her, and she may begin to hide whenever her need arises. Instead, gently pick her up and carry her to the proper location. It's inevitable that you'll get splashed a few times before the training period is over, so you might want to wear shorts or old clothing around the house for the first few weeks.

When your pup uses the papers properly, praise her. She needs to learn that the papers are a safe place to relieve herself. To encourage her to continue using the papers, keep a small piece of the soiled paper with the new, fresh papers. As your pup learns to use the papers, slowly decrease the papers until they cover only a small area.

The newspapers serve as a protective measure for your home; they shouldn't be a substitute for taking your pup outdoors. Consistency is vital; put your pup on a schedule. Take her outdoors first thing in the morning, after her nap, after feedings, after playtime, and before she goes to sleep. Always take her to the same spot in the yard so she begins to associate that area with this task. The odor, too, will stimulate a response. And always praise your puppy when the deed is done. Positive reinforcement is the best way to train your dog.

Accidents will inevitably occur, so prepare to take them in stride. If you catch your puppy in the middle of an accident, don't whisk her off to the newspapers in a rush. Say *no* firmly, not angrily. Never hit a pup for a mishap. Relieving herself is a biological function, like a baby soiling diapers. After your reprimand, pick her up—be gentle, not angry—and take her to the papers. Say *yes* in a positive tone, reinforcing good behavior. Only through our consistent behavior and reinforcement can a pup learn to associate a specific behavior with a positive or negative response.

Experts agree that it is useless to scold a puppy for having an accident or to rub her nose in the mess. This is especially true if you discover the accident later rather than catching the puppy in the act. Dogs simply cannot make the connection

Put your pup on a schedule, and always remember to take her outside first thing in the morning and right before bedtime.

between their "mistake" and the punishment they receive after the fact.

During housebreaking, give your pup plenty of praise and affection. Be aware of her behavior and try to interpret her needs before accidents happen; this sets the foundation for a loving and loyal relationship.

Basic Training Tips

Your puppy's first training began in the litter when she learned from her mother where to eat, where to sleep, and where to urinate. But unlike her mother, you can't be with your puppy twenty-four hours a day. What this means is that changing some behaviors will always take longer than you would like. You'll need to muster all your patience, so that no matter how many times you catch your pup chewing the sofa pillows, you'll be able to respond in a way that promotes learning. Patience combined with consistency and understanding will produce a well-behaved and happy dog who will be a delightful addition to your family.

A practical and effective training approach is positive reinforcement. As with paper-training, when your dog does what is expected, consistently reward her with praise or a treat. Positive reinforcement socializes a dog to be obedient. If the dog does what is expected, she will be rewarded. The behavior pattern is set. On the other hand, when you use punitive approaches such as swatting or frightening your dog, she will learn only to avoid doing that behavior when you're around. You also become the "punisher" in the dog's eyes—a person to be feared at certain times. This inconsistent role can undermine your training efforts. Although certain deterrence approaches are necessary in training, they should be coupled with plenty of positive reinforcement.

To alter unwanted behavior, you need to use a consistent response. This can be a simple command such as *no*. A mistake

Praise, praise, praise! Positive reinforcement breeds positive training results while you earn your puppy's trust and devotion.

that many owners make is using complex commands such as, "Towser, get off the couch. Off. No." This command is long, complex, and probably varies from incident to incident. From the tone of voice, your dog may get the idea, but will she associate the command with unwanted behavior?

The point of training your dog is to get her to associate a command with a specific type of behavior. A simple command such as *no*, used consistently, will get through to your dog: *no* means bad behavior; stop. There's no need to punish the dog physically if you're consistent and patient. Even a swat on the nose with the newspaper is unnecessary; besides, it's not usually effective.

Timing is crucial in training. You must catch your dog in the act of bad behavior—urinating on the carpet, chewing the pil-

Now would be a good time for this puppy to learn the word no.

lows, or scratching at the door—in order to reprimand her and ultimately change her behavior. Coming home an hour after the deed, showing your dog the scene of the crime, and then punishing her is confusing to the dog. Your puppy might understand that a chewed pillow is bad, but now she might chew pillows only when you're not home.

Dogs make simple associations: chewing pillows is bad behavior; not chewing pillows is good behavior. They're not capable of spiteful acts, such as chewing pillows because they have been left alone in the house. Although it seems at times that they *must* be misbehaving on purpose, most often these acts are inspired by anxiety, not revenge or anger. And puppies don't wait until you're gone to misbehave; they simply haven't yet made the association that when you are gone, pillows should not be chewed. This is a critical point to understand if you want to train your dog successfully. To change a dog's behavior, punishment should only be given when the dog is caught in the act. This way she will begin to understand the behavior you expect of her.

Each dog learns at her own rate. Be patient while your puppy learns good behavior from bad.

Sometimes we're unrealistic about how long it should take a dog to learn obedient behavior. Individual dogs have different temperaments and learning abilities, and some breeds adapt quickly and learn faster than others. Don't despair if your dog seems unresponsive at first; this doesn't necessarily mean she will never meet your expectations.

Obedience school is a fun way for you and your dog to learn.

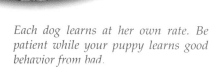

There are plenty of helpful books and videotapes available if you run into trouble training your pet, and if those don't work, you can always turn to a professional trainer. Many owners enroll their dogs in obedience classes. These classes are not only invaluable in teaching your dog the basic rules of behavior, they're a great way to meet other dog owners. You can make a few friends, team up with someone for evening walks, or exchange dog-sitting favors when you need to go out of town.

Establishing the Rules of the House

Sometimes it's harder for people to consistently follow house rules than it is for your pup or new dog. If you follow the rules inconsistently, your dog will too. Getting you and your dog on track begins with a solid schedule.

In setting a schedule, be realistic. If you're a late riser, will you really get up at six every morning and take your dog for her morning walk? Can you be home every evening by six to feed her? If duties will be shared among family members, will everyone follow through? These are issues that you and your family should discuss before your dog arrives. The key to a successful and consistent schedule is finding a balance between your dog's needs and your family's lifestyle.

This boy is taking the responsibility of caring for his dog seriously—and he's having fun!

Start by determining your puppy's daily needs. Keep in mind that your puppy will need to relieve herself right after waking up, eating, and playing no matter what time of day (or night) it is. Young puppies eat four times a day. And you'll want to set aside time for at least two walks a day.

Next, decide which family member is responsible for each task. If tasks are shared, post a schedule and make family members stick to it. Youngsters who forget to feed or exercise their pet should be made to realize how important it is that they follow through on their dog's basic needs. But don't be surprised if the majority of dog-related chores end up falling on an adult's shoulders.

Giving your dog the love and care she needs should be a priority. Your dog depends on you for feeding and exercise. If you leave an active dog cooped up in a house all day, you'll end up with an agitated, ill-behaved animal. That's why it's so important to get a dog whose temperament suits your lifestyle. For example, retrievers live to retrieve, so don't buy a golden retriever because you love her coat, then refuse to give her what she needs: balls, Frisbees, or sticks to retrieve, and a lot of time with someone willing to toss them.

Even if your dog is left outside all day and is free to run and explore, she still needs a regular feeding schedule and plenty of companionship. When many new owners discover they

Your puppy will begin to depend on her feeding routine.

Dog Nutrition

The staggering array of dog foods available in pet stores and supermarkets can be daunting for a novice dog owner. To avoid the confusion, ask your vet and breeder to suggest several brands of food. Commercial dog foods are usually broken down into three categories: puppy, adult, and geriatric.

Instill good eating habits in your puppy from the very beginning by never feeding her at the table and by limiting the amount of "people food" she eats to no more than 10 percent of her diet.

Feeding your dog table scraps can turn an obedient pet into a beggar or a finicky eater. A treat every now and then is fine, but be careful not to overdo it.

Obesity is a tragic problem for many dogs. Overweight dogs die earlier, are less healthy, and are less energetic than other dogs. For some breeds such as dachshunds the extra weight can cause back problems. If your dog seems too hefty, consult your vet about special low-fat diets and exercise regimens that will get your pet back in shape.

can't find time for their pet, it's heartbreaking for both owner and dog.

One routine your dog will depend on is her feeding schedule. Feed your dog in the same place and approximately at the same time every day. Puppies need to eat four times a day until they are about four months old, at which point three meals daily is enough. At six months, puppies need only two meals a day. After a year, they can get by on a single feeding, but many people prefer to divide the daily fare up into two meals. Always have plenty of fresh water available.

Do not feed your dog at the table—she will become a beggar. Begging is an extremely annoying trait; the "cuteness" of a begging dog wears off quickly. Unfortunately, it can be difficult to break your dog of the begging habit once it has taken hold. Soon she'll be begging everywhere, not just at the table. And anything that relates to a tidbit the dog has successfully begged—the sound of the toaster, the refrigerator door opening—can result in your dog underfoot, begging.

It seems that children love to see a dog beg, so if you have kids you should be very firm about the no-begging rule. Teach your children to give the dog a treat only as a reward or at special times such as before bed. Dog treats are an excellent tool for positive reinforcement when you are training your dog, but they will lose their effectiveness if your pet knows she can beg one anytime.

Kids and Dogs: Made for Each Other

Children and dogs make great companions. Kids are instinctively drawn to dogs, whose desire for affection and attention so closely matches their own. But youngsters need to be taught compassion. They learn this trait mainly from their parents. Showing a youngster how to lovingly and responsibly care for a pet is a wonderful way to teach respect and compassion for other living creatures.

Children need to be taught the proper way to handle a dog. Once learned, though, dog and child can become the best of friends.

Set Ground Rules for Your Children

1. Teach your children the difference between playing and teasing.

🐕 Yelling or dancing around a confined dog is cruel to the dog and dangerous for children.

🐕 Never pull a dog's tail, ears, or legs, and never strike her while playing.

🐕 Respect a dog's privacy and turf: When your dog retreats to her crate or tries to escape the kids' clutches, children must be taught not to chase the dog down.

2. Teach your children safe training techniques.

🐕 Never hit a dog to punish her.

🐕 Teach youngsters the same basic training commands you use.

3. Teach your children to share in the care of the family pet.

🐕 Put your children on a schedule, making them responsible for feeding, walking, grooming, taking the dog outdoors to relieve herself, and cleaning up the yard or dog run.

🐕 Your children should be involved in activities such as bathing the dog and going to the vet.

🐕 Kids should be taught to report any unusual behavior in their pet, such as limping or excessive scratching.

These lessons should begin long before you bring your new dog home. Give your kids plenty of opportunities to interact with pets at friends' homes, animal shelters, or pet stores. Always supervise these interactions, and notice how each of your children responds to animals. Are they fearful? Considerate? Do they play roughly with the animal? Noting your children's behavior with animals will help you predict how they will respond to a new pet.

Some dogs can be infinitely forgiving of a child's rough-and-tumble treatment. If you're lucky (and have purchased an even-tempered breed), your dog will patiently endure having her ears tugged, fur pulled, and tail yanked by a curious toddler. But responsible parents and loving owners don't take such chances. Parents need to teach children how to care for animals properly in order to protect their pets from potentially dangerous encounters. To get your children off to the right start, set ground rules for them.

Puppies are fragile and require special care, especially around small children and toddlers. A small child should be sitting on the floor when holding a puppy. Have the child wrap one of his or her arms around the puppy's chest and the other arm under the pup's front legs. Be sure that all interactions between a young child and pet are supervised by an adult.

Older children who can understand and follow the ground rules will usually form a deep, abiding attachment to the family dog. As many a grateful parent has discovered, kids and dogs can keep each other occupied for hours. It's likely that no matter how fervently children plead with parents to buy a puppy, the parents will have to do some nagging to get their youngsters to share in daily tasks. But parents will probably never have to nag children to love or play with a pet. That comes naturally, and that, after all, is the most important part about owning a dog.

This little girl knows the safest way to hold her puppy.

The Health of Your Dog

6

Y ou and your dog are about to embark on a long relationship. Depending on the breed, dogs live anywhere from ten to twenty years. To keep your pet fit and healthy, you'll want to enlist the aid of an experienced veterinarian and learn the basics of canine health care. The first step is to select your vet.

Teaming Up with the Right Veterinarian

There are plenty of reliable sources for veterinarian referrals, among them your puppy's breeder, local kennel clubs, obedience trainers, and friends or neighbors who own dogs. Animal shelters are also a good resource, as they frequently have a list of vets who volunteer to help in the shelter's programs. These veterinarians are likely to be conscientious and caring people.

When you have the names of two or three vets, call and arrange to meet them at their clinics. During this visit, you'll be able to assess the vet's demeanor toward clients and animals. A good vet is gentle and loving with animals and responsive to owners' questions. The staff should be courteous and helpful as well.

While you're meeting with prospective veterinarians, ask each of them their opinion of the breed you intend to buy. You may get lucky and find a vet who is especially enthusiastic about your breed or who can offer useful advice or caveats before you bring your pet home.

Factors to Consider when Choosing a Vet

Location: Your vet should be relatively close to your home, in case you have to rush your pet there in an emergency.

Expense: Veterinarian care is somewhat expensive, although costs vary from region to region. Call several vets in your area and inquire about basic fees to get a sense of the going rate in your area. You may wish to purchase animal health insurance to cover major illnesses or surgeries, which cost thousands of dollars.

Emergency Service: Ask if twenty-four-hour emergency service is available and who is on call to provide coverage on weekends and holidays.

Hospitalization and Home Visits: Inquire about the vet's policy regarding hospitalization: in many cases, it's preferable to treat a sick animal at home, where he's in familiar surroundings. Also ask if the vet makes house calls in case of extreme emergencies.

Cleanliness: All reputable vets will allow you to tour the clinic and treatment areas. Both should be clean and warm, as should the kennel where the animals are housed.

Clinic Ambience: Popular vets often have tight schedules, but there's no excuse for making pets and owners wait for hours or for not maintaining a clean, comfortable waiting area. Do the people waiting seem relaxed, or are they irritated? Does the office appear to be functioning smoothly, or is it disorganized? Is the staff friendly, or do they brush off your inquiries? There are plenty of vets around, so make sure you choose one whose clinic seems to be professionally run.

Your Dog's First Visit to the Vet

Whether you've purchased a puppy or an adult dog, you'll want to pay a visit to the vet within two or three days of bringing him home. Your adult dog's first vet visit includes booster shots, as well as the typical annual checkup, including a heartworm test and advice from the vet on preventive medication, nutrition, exercise, and any other problems your dog may be experiencing.

This first checkup is particularly important for pups, who will need to continue to visit the vet every two to four weeks until they are four to six months old. During this time, your puppy should receive a series of vaccinations to protect him against diseases such as rabies, canine distemper, infectious canine hepatitis, leptospirosis, kennel cough, and parvovirus. All of these vaccinations require annual booster shots with the exception of some rabies vaccines, which may require a booster every three years.

Although your new puppy should come with a health guarantee, the vet will examine him extensively to determine if he has any hereditary or congenital defects or any infectious diseases.

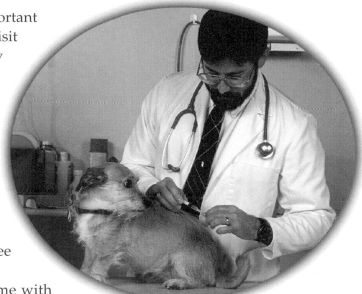

Vaccinations and yearly boosters help keep your dog protected from disease.

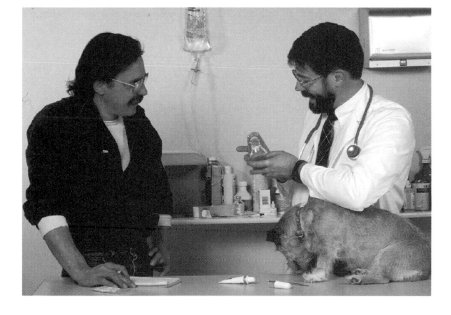

Choose a vet you feel comfortable talking to and who'll answer your questions clearly.

Spaying and Neutering—An Act of Love

Unless you plan to breed your dog, you should have her or him spayed or neutered. Spaying and neutering is standard

practice for caring dog owners and is the first line of defense against canine overpopulation. There are few sadder sights than a litter of unwanted puppies being delivered to an animal shelter—puppies who will have three or four short days to captivate a possible owner before they are euthanized.

Some people are concerned that spaying or neutering is not "natural," that it will alter their pet's temperament. The operation *will* affect your pet's behavior—for the better. Intact male dogs (unneutered) are considerably more territorial and prone to wandering than neutered males. The scent

Some of the More Common Genetic Defects and Infectious Diseases

🐕 **Stenotic Nares:** A condition in which the nostril openings are too small, making it difficult for the dog to breathe normally. It usually occurs in flat-faced breeds such as bulldogs and pugs.

🐕 **Bite Abnormalities:** The bite refers to the way a dog's teeth fit together when his mouth is closed. The norm for the bite varies according to breed, and the vet can determine if your pet falls within the normal range or has an overshot or undershot jaw.

🐕 **Hydrocephalus:** An abnormal accumulation of cerebrospinal fluid around the brain

🐕 **Eye Defects:** Some breeds are more susceptible than others to eye problems such as cataracts and retinal degeneration. Your vet may recommend that you also visit a veterinary ophthalmologist.

🐕 **Heart Defects:** Some heart defects are extremely serious; others are minor or correctable.

🐕 **Hernias:** A hernia is a weakness in the abdominal muscle wall through which the abdominal contents protrude, causing a lump. If the area of weakness becomes large, it's possible for intestine to poke through, a situation that may be life threatening. The most common areas for hernias in a puppy are around the navel and the groin.

🐕 **Cryptorchidism:** A condition in which one or both of a puppy's testicles do not descend (in normal pups, the testicles descend within ten days of birth). Testicles that are retained in a pup's abdomen or inguinal canal are more prone to cancer. Surgery to remove them can be difficult, and the healing time is longer than in a normal neuter.

🐕 **Intestinal Parasites:** Roundworms and tapeworms, among other intestinal parasites, can deplete the nutrients your puppy consumes. The vet will ask you to bring a sample of your puppy's stool to be tested for these parasites.

🐕 **External Parasites:** Fleas, lice, or mange mites can make your puppy's life miserable and will probably go after you as well. The vet will ask you if your pup has been scratching his ears or body, a sign of external parasites.

of a dog in heat will send the intact male off on a ceaseless love quest, forcing you to chase after him repeatedly or listen to his incessant barking and clawing at your fence. His social graces leave much to be desired as well. Intact males are very fond of licking their genitals, "humping" people's legs, sniffing every hydrant and bush, and fighting with other dogs. Their aggressive behavior sometimes extends to people, too. It's vital to realize that male puppies must be neutered *before* these behaviors appear. After these traits have developed in a male dog, neutering often does not change the behavior.

Unspayed females also display behavior that most dog owners would prefer to avoid. They, like intact males, may become territorial, and as their cycles wane and wax, they can be unpredictable. Most pet owners are unprepared for the messiness of their female's heat cycle and are truly shocked by the collection of unwanted suitors howling and fighting along the perimeters of their property.

If the above arguments aren't enough to convince you to spay or neuter your dog, the tremendous health benefits will surely persuade you. In males, neutering helps prevent hormone-related diseases such as infections or cancer of the prostate and perianal adenomas. Neutered males cannot contract testicular cancer, since their testicles are removed.

In females, the many health advantages are even more pronounced. The intact female goes through two heats a year, during which hormones alter her body to prepare it for pregnancy. If she is not bred, she still experiences a "false pregnancy": her uterus swells and her teats may fill with milk. In the wild, this phenomenon ensures that all the pups in a pack will have a teat to nurse from, even if their own mother dies. For domestic dogs, going into heat twice a year has no such redeeming features. Instead, it puts the dog at higher risk for pyometra, a serious infection of the uterus, and for mammary cancer, which claims the lives of many female dogs each year. Puppies who are spayed before they ever go into heat are at very low risk for mammary cancer, and spayed females cannot get uterine diseases because the uterus is removed.

What about the old maxim that spayed and neutered animals get fat and lazy? The procedure does not cause obesity; dog owners who feed their pets too much are the root of that

Unneutered male dogs sometimes exhibit aggressive behavior along with other undesirable traits. A neutered dog makes a better, healthier, and happier pet.

problem. Neutered males are less likely to roam or fight, both of which burn calories, but that in itself will not cause a healthy dog to gain weight. As for laziness, all dogs' metabolism slows as they mature. Fortunately for their owners, even the most

Shelters are overflowing with homeless pets waiting to be adopted or euthanized. It is important to prevent unwanted pregnancies through spaying and neutering.

excitable two year old will eventually slow down, whether or not he or she is fixed.

Puppies can be spayed or neutered as young as eight weeks, although most vets prefer to wait until the dog is about six months old. Older dogs can undergo the operation, but as noted above, behavioral and health benefits may be greatly diminished.

The procedure takes place in the vet's office with the dog under anesthesia. Neutering rarely requires an overnight stay. Although your pup might be groggy when he first comes home, after a good night's sleep and a little food he will most likely be as bouncy as usual. Vets usually recommend that females being spayed stay overnight. When you get your spayed pup home, the biggest challenge is to restrain her from being too active and from licking her stitches. When you leave the clinic after the procedure, ask the vet if he or she can recommend a substance for you to dab on the stitch area to discourage your dog from licking. The vet will remove the stitches in ten to fourteen days or they will fall out on their own, depending on the type of suture material that was used.

Refrain from playing roughly with spayed or neutered pets for about a week, but feel free to leash-walk them.

Despite the many advantages, some people resist the idea of spaying and neutering their dogs. Their reasons are most often based on a misunderstanding of the domestic dog's nature and needs or a misguided desire to breed the family pet. But breeding demands a serious commitment of time, effort, and money and rarely nets the breeder much profit.

Health Warning Signs

After the first four to six months of his life, your pup will see the vet only once a year for a checkup. Between visits, it will be up to you to notice signs of distress or illness in your dog.

Dogs do not get colds or the flu, so symptoms such as coughing, vomiting, diarrhea, and listlessness may indicate a serious problem. Coughing can indicate either a minor case of kennel cough or a more serious affliction such as heartworm. To be on the safe side, call the vet if coughing persists for more than twenty-four hours. Likewise, call if your pet is listless or won't eat for a day or two, especially if these symptoms are accompanied by diarrhea or vomiting. If your dog has diarrhea, or constipation lasts for more than twenty-four hours, call the vet. Blood in the stool is another danger sign—contact the vet immediately. You should also call the vet if your dog vomits

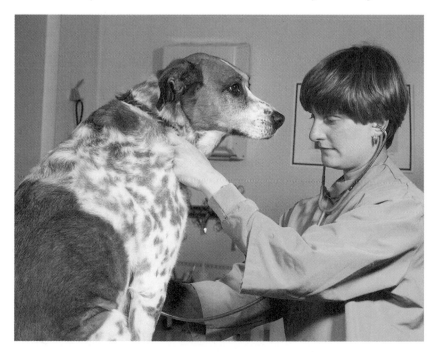

This vet is examining a dog during his annual checkup.

more than two or three times in a twenty-four-hour period, or if he vomits for more than two or three days.

Many dogs develop some lumps and bumps, particularly as they get older. Often these are abscesses that can be lanced by the vet, but sometimes they are tumors. As is the case with people, the sooner a tumor is removed the better. A lump should be checked by a vet within thirty-six hours of detection, especially if it is tender to the touch.

Your vet may prescribe eye drops if your dog's eyes are red and runny.

Redness in your dog's eyes or ears may indicate an inflammation, an infection, or both. See the vet if your pet's eyes are runny, cloudy, or filled with matter, or if you notice discharge or excess wax in his ears. Any unusual discharge from your dog's nose, mouth, rectum, or genitals should be checked as well.

An increase in your dog's thirst or urination is also cause for concern. If it continues for more than twenty-four hours, call the vet. If your pet stops urinating, the situation is equally grave; he may have a urinary blockage or be dehydrated.

If you've vigilantly cared for your dog throughout his youth and young adulthood, his chances of living to a happy old age are greatly improved. But dogs slow down when they get older and become much less tolerant of change. Your older dog will sleep a lot and in general be less curious than he was as a youngster. Like people, older dogs tend to be forgetful and feel most comfortable sticking to a structured daily routine. A geriatric dog can become quite agitated if kenneled or hospitalized.

Dogs over seven years old should have a checkup every six months. As your dog ages, he'll become more susceptible to several ailments. He may experience a loss of vision. Hazy vision and cataracts are not unusual in older dogs. If their senses of hearing and smell are still strong, they tend to tolerate the loss of vision fairly well.

As they age, many dogs experience some degree of kidney failure, making it difficult for them to excrete concentrated urine. They must drink more water and urinate more frequently. Do not cut down on the dog's water supply in order to keep him from having accidents in the house: lack of adequate water could lead to kidney failure. Instead, make sure he has plenty of opportunities to relieve himself. Now may be the time to install that dog door so Towser won't have to wait for you every time he needs to urinate. Ask your vet about special diets that can help older dogs with this problem.

Constipation caused by lack of exercise, poor diet, and the generally diminished physical capabilities of the older dog, is another ailment your dog might suffer. Daily exercise, a high-fiber diet, stool softeners, and laxatives all can help the problem. Ask your vet for suggestions.

It's essential that dogs over eight years old get daily exercise to keep their muscles toned, their joints flexible, and their weight down. Exercise will improve your dog's mood, too, just as it does with people. Ask your vet about the proper amount

Regular exercise, a good diet, and play-time keep your older dog feeling young and healthy.

of exercise for your breed. Older dogs should also be fed a "senior" diet; many brands are available at pet stores.

Dogs are not complainers—they seem somewhat impervious to discomfort, which makes it all the more important that you notice when something's amiss. You know your dog better than anyone, and you can pick up on subtle changes in his attitude. If you believe there may be a problem, don't hesitate to call your vet. Often a brief conversation will ease your anxiety, and sometimes that extra bit of caution can save your pet's life.

Dental Health

Once a year, your dog should have his teeth checked by a vet, who may recommend that they be professionally cleaned. The rest of the time, you'll need to help keep his teeth strong and healthy by brushing them at home, usually about twice a week. Ask your vet how much brushing is appropriate for your dog and what type of veterinary toothpaste is best. Dogs cannot use human toothpaste: they don't like the taste or the foaminess, and it can upset their stomach. You can brush your dog's teeth with a soft child's toothbrush, a brush designed for pets, or a finger brush.

Providing your dog with proper chew toys is an important part of his dental hygiene. Do not give your dog hard nylon bones or knuckle bones to chew on. These are too hard and can lead to dead teeth. As a general rule, your dog should chew on items that are softer than his own teeth and are slightly abrasive to help remove plaque.

Dry dog food is definitely the best choice for healthy teeth and gums. The abrasive quality helps remove plaque,

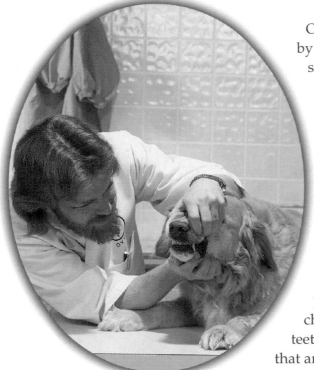

Annual dental checkups will help keep your dog's teeth and gums free of disease.

Regularly brushing your dog's teeth will help keep them healthy through your pet's old age. That's something to smile about.

whereas moist or canned dog food tends to work its way into the crevices of the dog's teeth along the gum line.

Canine First Aid

Over the course of a lifetime, most dogs have their fair share of mishaps—heartstroke, insect bites, cuts, and bruises. All but the more minor of these cases warrant a trip to the vet, but you may also need to provide emergency first aid.

When a dog is in pain or frightened, he may bite, so it's a good idea to keep a muzzle handy for these emergencies. If you don't have one, you can make one out of a necktie, leash, or any piece of fabric that's at least 2 feet long. Make a large loop and tie it firmly around the dog's muzzle so that he can't open his mouth. Bring the two ends along each side of the dog's head and behind the ears, then tie them at the back of his head. Don't make it too tight. Although the muzzle won't inhibit the dog's breathing, it could cut off his circulation. As soon as you complete the first aid procedure and you feel confident that your dog won't hurt you, remove the muzzle.

Acute Emergency!

If your dog experiences any of the following life-threatening symptoms, administer first aid if called for, then phone the vet immediately or drive directly to the clinic:

✚ Bloating of the abdomen with retching (gastric torsion)

✚ Bulging eyeball

✚ Choking or gasping for air

✚ Fainting or convulsions

✚ Foaming at the mouth, abnormal drooling, slobbering

✚ Sudden loss of coordination or balance; staggering

✚ Sudden vomiting or diarrhea and change in behavior

✚ Swelling of the head, face, or limbs

Keep wounds clean with soap and water, and rush any dog with possible broken bones to the vet.

Remember, all of the techniques below are meant to be used as emergency measures to ease your dog's discomfort before a trip to the vet. They are not intended as a substitute for veterinary care. At the very least, call your vet as soon as you've administered the first aid to report the situation and get instructions.

Burns can be caused by either heat or chemical substances. For heat burns, apply a cold compress immediately and leave on for up to half an hour. Do not treat the burn with greasy ointments, butter, or other kinds of grease. Your vet may prescribe an antibiotic. For chemical burns, flood the area with water and call the vet immediately for advice.

If you find your dog choking, restrain him by wrapping him in a heavy blanket. Try to remove the object with your fingers or pliers. Do not pull on a string or thread—there could be a needle or some other sharp object attached to it. Call the vet at once.

Don't use alcohol or an antiseptic on cuts and other wounds. Instead, clean the wound with soap and water. Apply a loose bandage. See a vet if the wound is longer than an inch or two and deeper than a scrape. For severe bleeding, wrap the wound firmly and apply only enough pressure to stop the bleeding. Loosen the bandage every eight minutes. Do not apply a tourniquet. See the vet immediately.

If you suspect your dog has frostbite, warm the frozen appendages with tepid water (about 90 degrees F/32 degrees C) and massage gently with a towel. The frostbitten parts should thaw within ten minutes; call the vet as soon as possible.

Heatstroke is an ever-present danger in warm months and a reason you should never leave a dog in a warm, parked car. Symptoms include fever, shock, drooling, panting, and a rapid pulse. Lower the dog's temperature by hosing him down or immersing him in cool water. When his body temperature reaches normal (101.5 degrees F/38.5 degrees C), remove him from the water. Give him small amounts of water to replace lost body fluids.

Insect bites and stings may be treated with the same ointments you'd use to treat yourself. However, some dogs have allergic reactions such as swelling that would require a rush trip to the vet. Watch your dog closely if he's been stung to make sure he's not experiencing such a reaction.

Do not try to treat a poisoned animal yourself—rush him to the vet. Some common poisons are antifreeze, gasoline products, pest and rodent killers, and household cleaners. They can cause convulsions, retching, and trembling in your dog. Do not try to pour medicine down his throat or make him throw up, either of which could make the situation worse. Just get to a vet, quickly.

Your dog can go into shock if he's been badly injured. Symptoms include dilated pupils, shallow breathing, cold and clammy skin, and pale mucous membranes. Wrap him in a warm blanket, try to keep him calm and still, and take him to the vet immediately.

A dog who is looked after by an attentive and knowledgeable person and receives the proper veterinary care is likely to live to a ripe old age. But caring for your dog goes far beyond making sure he gets his yearly checkups and eats a nutritious diet. The reason most people buy dogs is for the companionship, and the very best way to make sure your relationship will be rewarding for both of you is to begin training your dog when he is an eager-to-please puppy.

Some dogs are allergic to flea bites. Flea spray is only one of the many flea-control products available to keep your dog flea free. Talk to your vet about the many others.

Training and Showing Your Dog

7

The minute your dog sets foot inside your home, she will eagerly begin to absorb the sights, sounds, smells, and social relationships of all the people in her world. With startling acuity, dogs will grasp who has the most power within a family and often try to take advantage of "subordinates."

Dogs are opportunistic by nature. They will quickly claim their favorite place to sleep, even if it happens to be yours as well. They'll locate the food and the garbage. Most people marvel at their dog's intuition — you could be sitting on the couch, just thinking of going out, and suddenly your dog is standing in front of you waving her tail expectantly. The cues dogs pay attention to are often too subtle for us to recognize.

A dog's perceptive nature, intelligence, and natural desire to pursue her own interests are what makes her such an amusing and responsive pet. But her lively temperament can also be a challenge to a new dog owner. Unless you provide structure for your dog, your home life can quickly dissolve into chaos. Because dogs are pack animals who feel safe and secure when there is order and routine within their group, a trained dog is a happy dog. And a happy dog has a happy owner.

Training 101

Everyone has encountered that unruly canine who jumps on people, drags her owner down the street, steals food, and runs in the opposite direction when her name is called. Thousands of perfectly nice dogs end up making one-way trips to the animal shelter because their owners perceive them as incorrigible. Although some dogs are naturally more excitable than others, most seemingly insurmountable problems can be overcome with proper training. Owners who view their dogs as incorrigible may not realize that they, too, play a part in the dynamic. Dogs need to be trained. If they aren't, they can't be held entirely responsible for their unruly or disobedient behavior.

Once you've trained your puppy to follow the basic rules of your house, you'll want to expand her schooling so that you can take her anywhere, confident that she will behave properly. Training is essentially the same for puppies and adult dogs, although you must be very gentle with a puppy and remember that she has a shorter attention span than an adult. Training your dog does not have to be especially time-consuming or difficult; obedience classes usually meet once a week for an hour and your training sessions take only about fifteen minutes a day. And if you're enthusiastic about your new pet, you'll probably enjoy that time together.

There are various levels of training, beginning with walking on a leash and proceeding to advanced field and obedience trials. But all successful training contains the same three building blocks to a reliable performance: consistency, quick corrections, and praise. If you have a puppy, you'll need to start with collar and leash breaking.

Put a soft buckle collar on your puppy, leaving enough room to get a couple of fingers beneath the strap. The pup will scratch at the collar frequently at first but should quickly become accustomed to it. Check the collar weekly; puppies grow so rapidly that collars can become too tight practically overnight.

Once the puppy is comfortable with her collar, you can snap on the leash. Let the puppy drag the leash for an hour or two at a time, feeling the weight of it, tripping on it a bit, even

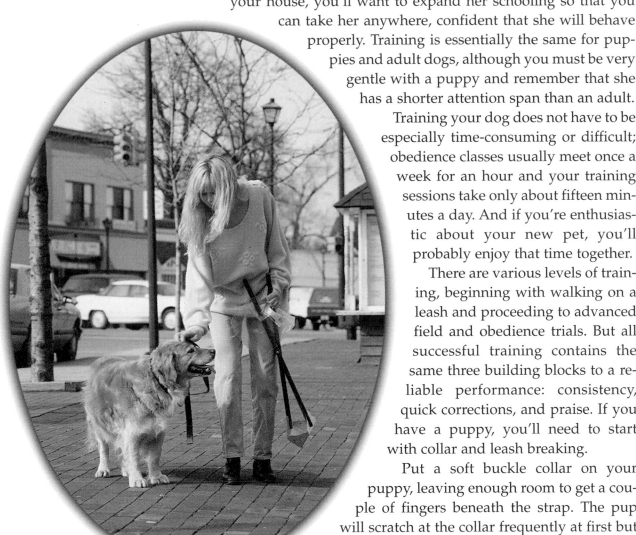

A well-trained dog is a pleasure to be with.

picking it up in her mouth. Never leave a leash on an unsupervised dog; it may snag or get tangled on something, causing your puppy to panic or even choke. When your puppy accepts the leash and is no longer bothered by its presence, you are ready for controlled walking.

The purpose of controlled walking is to teach a dog to pay attention to the person at the end of the leash and to follow in the same direction. The exercise is the same for puppies and older dogs, but again, remember to be extra gentle and encouraging with a puppy.

Gently encourage your puppy to follow you during controlled walking; as always, remember to praise her for a job well done.

With the dog on a loose leash, walk briskly away, calling her name, patting your thigh encouragingly, and keeping up a happy patter of talk. The dog should follow with interest. Change directions frequently, particularly any time the dog gets distracted. Your change in direction will pull the dog back toward you again. Don't yank on the leash of a young puppy, but older dogs can be given a quick tug. The instant the dog moves toward you, praise her lavishly and keep up the encouragement. A dog who is reluctant to follow can usually be convinced with a tidbit of food. This is especially helpful with puppies, who get distracted easily. Practice this exercise for a few minutes each day, and your dog will soon understand that you are in control when she is on a leash. You are now ready for more formal obedience training.

Obedience Class vs. Training at Home

All dogs should learn a few basic commands: *sit, down, stay, heel, and come.* The commands *off* (to curb jumping) and *leave it* (for "get away from that!") are also quite useful. The commands are easy to teach but often difficult to enforce, especially for the novice trainer. It's common to hear owners of unruly dogs sheepishly insist, "She always obeys at home." Unfortunately, if she doesn't obey away from home, she's not really trained.

Most home-trained dogs fail to follow commands in public because they've been trained in isolation. Home training does not prepare them for situations in the real world, where minding you can be a matter of life and death. Particularly if you've had experience handling dogs, you can certainly give home training a try. You can find books in pet stores and libraries devoted specifically to obedience training. They are excellent references to have on hand, whether or not you do your training on your own. However, the best place to train your dog is at a good obedience school, where she will learn that she must mind you in spite of the presence of other dogs and innumerable distractions.

Some experienced dog owners prefer to home train their dogs.

Every dog has her quirks, and some commands will be more difficult to teach than others. Your trainer can explain your dog's behavior and assist you through the rough spots so that you don't give up in frustration. The trainer can also alert you to your own body language; you may be unwittingly sending your dog signals that could hamper the training process.

Training in a group class has additional benefits for both you and your dog. Working in a group setting will keep you motivated to follow through on your lessons—there's a healthy comradeship among dog owners. As an added bonus, your dog will get the valuable socialization she needs to be well adapted among people and other dogs.

Many good trainers advertise in the telephone book, at pet stores, and at grooming parlors. Ask a friend with a well-trained dog for a recommendation. Dog training is one of those services that is not regulated, so you must be an informed con-

Training your dog at an obedience school gives you easy access to knowledgeable trainers and continues your dog's socialization.

sumer. That means you'll want to interview trainers before deciding on enrolling in an obedience class.

When interviewing potential trainers, ask how long they have been training dogs, where they received their experience, and if they have experience training your breed of dog. If a trainer makes any sarcastic or disparaging remarks about your breed, it's best to use someone else. Ask each trainer about the methods and philosophy used in the classes. Dogs can be successfully trained through a variety of methods, but if you're not comfortable with a trainer's ideology, select a different trainer. You might also ask about a challenging behavior problem you're having with your dog. An astute trainer has creative solutions and is also aware that one solution does not fit all dogs. Finally, ask to observe a class. Notice how much assistance each person is receiving from the trainer; if the classes are too big, the students may not be getting their money's worth. Take the time to notice if the dogs and their owners are enjoying themselves. Training a dog should be fun for both of you.

Some dog owners are skeptical about the need for formal obedience training for a dog who is only a home companion. Other owners fear that obedience training will "break a dog's spirit." On the contrary, obedience training is truly a bonding experience between dog and owner. Your dog will gain respect for you as the boss and will be comfortable with your role.

Training methods used nowadays are almost always positive in approach; there is nothing harsh or cruel about them.

The Basic Commands

When you consider all the daily interactions you have with your dog, it's obvious that simple obedience commands will make the difference between chaos and order. Having a dog sit for her dinner or for her leash is better than having her leap through the air in anticipation. Having a dog lay down on the floor and stay there while company is present allows her to remain with the group rather than be banished due to her annoying and busy nose. Having a dog heel on a crowded city street is far more appropriate than having her lunge in front of unwary pedestrians. And lastly, training your dog to wait at corners, at doors, or before leaping out of cars is essential for her safety. Dogs are truly creatures of routine. They won't feel thwarted by obeying commands. In fact, most dogs will find the commands reassuring as they establish their place in your world.

Individual dogs and individual breeds vary in the amount of time they need to learn commands. Temperament also plays a part in how difficult certain commands will be to learn. Excitable dogs have a hard time with the sit command. Dominant dogs struggle with the down command. As a trainer, you must remember to be patient and positive, and to keep your sense of humor.

For each lesson, have your dog wear a chain or nylon slip collar. Puppies under six months can wear a buckle collar. Always train your dog on a leash; a 6-foot leather or cotton web leash is best.

Teaching a dog to consistently obey the basic commands is essential for your sanity and the dog's. This well-behaved mixed breed is sitting patiently for her dinner.

Showing in Obedience Trials

Once you've been "bitten" by the obedience bug, you may enjoy competing in obedience trials. Obedience trials are usually run in conjunction with conformation dog shows, competitions judged on conformity to the particular standard of one's

Obedience trials are a fun and effective way for both owner and dog (in this case a Bernese mountain dog) to bond.

breed. Your dog must be intact (unspayed or unneutered) if you want your pet to compete in conformation showing, but all AKC obedience trials are open to altered pets, and novice trainers are encouraged to participate. Some areas have mix breed clubs that conduct their own obedience events as well. Contact the AKC or a dog trainer, or attend a local dog show to get information about rules and enrollment.

Three titles are awarded in obedience showing. Once earned, a title follows your dog's registered name on her pedigree. The titles are ranked by difficulty. A Companion Dog (CD) is earned for basic obedience. A Companion Dog Excellent (CDX) indicates mastery of retrieving and more difficult stays. The third level, Utility Dog (UD), is very advanced. To earn this title, dogs perform exercises in following hand signals, hurdle work, and scent discrimination. Utility work is exciting to watch and gives one a deep appreciation for the intelligence of dogs. To earn any of these titles, a dog must pass the same test three times at each level. A dog reliably trained in basic obedience can achieve a CD with little difficulty.

Conformation Showing

If your dog is an excellent example of her breed, you may want to show her in conformation as well as obedience. *Conformation* refers to the overall physical shape and attributes of a dog. In this type of event, the dog must learn to pose

Tips to Becoming an Effective Trainer

Your goal as a trainer is to have a dog who behaves reliably in any situation. The fundamental concept underlying all training techniques is consistency. The more consistent you are as a trainer, the more reliable your dog's behavior will be. No matter what training methods you employ, there are a few ground rules that will increase your effectiveness.

Give a command only once, then correct your dog by placing her in position. A common error is nagging the dog by repeating the same command over and over. If your dog does not obey on the first command, assume she does not know the command and correct her immediately. Show your dog (kindly and patiently) that you mean business; this will build reliability.

Praise, praise, praise! Too often we rely on the word *no* but give little information on what we expect. Praise tells our dogs that what they are doing is right and that we are pleased with them. Be liberal with praise, but be sure to praise your dog while she is performing the command, not after you've released her.

Never give commands to a dog who is out of control. If you yell commands to a dog who is running wild, she will quickly learn that she doesn't have to obey you.

Always go to your dog to make a correction. Never punish a dog who comes to you, no matter what mischief she has been making! If you do, your dog will learn to run away from you in anticipation of punishment.

Never train when you are frustrated or angry. Your dog is sensitive and will sense your displeasure. Training must be a positive experience. If you've reached an impasse, go back to an exercise the dog can do correctly, praise her, and call it a day. Always end on a high note.

Notice signs of fatigue in your dog. If your dog begins to lag, make yawnlike expressions, or roll over, she has reached her limit. Do one easy exercise and quit for the day. In general, keep lessons to about fifteen minutes a day.

Vary your training areas. Train at home, in parks, in parking lots, or while walking down the street. Also train in context; build in the routines of your household. Varying locations will expose your dog to many situations, reinforcing all the time that she must obey you anywhere, not only at home or in class.

Remember to have fun! Play with your dog before, during, and after training sessions. Training should be a rewarding experience for both of you; the more fun you make it, the more responsive your dog will be.

correctly for the judge's examination and must walk with the proper gait so that the judge can evaluate her movement and soundness.

For a championship title, a dog must earn 15 points in the conformation show ring by competing with other dogs of the same sex and breed. She can earn 0-5 points per show depending upon the number of the entries. During her show career, she must have two "majors," or shows that award at least 3 points to the winners. The title of "champion" will appear before your dog's registered name on her pedigree. A championship is considered a most prestigious title in the dog world, yet many champions are handled by amateurs and live the life of the family pet when out of the ring.

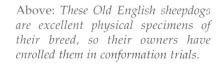

Obedience trials and conformation showing are only two avenues to gaining titles through specific training. Other events include scent tracking, hunt tests and field trials, agility course training, and *schutzhund* (protection) trials. Dogs are marvelously diverse and intelligent animals. When you begin to master the art of training your own dog, your teamwork may find its best expression in the gratifying world of shows and trials.

Above: *These Old English sheepdogs are excellent physical specimens of their breed, so their owners have enrolled them in conformation trials.*

Below: *This German shepherd and owner are participating in agility course competition—a fun and exciting way to challenge a dog's mind and body.*

Breeding Your Dog

8

No doubt about it: your dog is the most exemplary canine ever to grace a front porch. After a year or so of enjoying his playful disposition, astonishing intelligence, and breathtaking beauty, you're convinced that for the sake of the breed, this dog must produce offspring.

It's the rare dog lover who hasn't had a few fleeting thoughts about breeding his or her pet. But breeding a dog is a complicated process. What may seem like a fun family experience or an easy way to make a little extra money can turn into an expensive venture with time-consuming complications or, worse yet, puppies you can't sell. The amateur breeder is often left with several growing mouths to feed in a house that's not adequately set up for so many dogs. Besides, the average prices for stud fees run $300 to $500, and the stud owner often wants a pick puppy as well. For these reasons, it's extremely important to consider all aspects of the breeding experience before you make the decision to breed your dog.

Why Do You Want to Breed Your Dog?

Perhaps the most misunderstood aspect about breeding dogs is that you'll make money. The majority of professional breeders don't depend on dog sales for their income—they breed dogs out of a love for the particular breed. Consider the costs: a breeder must pay for stud fees, genetic screening, and

This male yellow Labrador retriever is a stud dog who is bred for his excellent conformation and temperament. He has been tested and found free of genetic diseases such as hip dysplasia.

general care and feeding of the brood bitch. And then there are the added costs of the litter.

Check with your city licensing department or animal control agency to find out if there are any breeding restrictions or kennel license requirements in your area and what the costs and procedures are. Call the AKC or another registration organization to find out the fees for registering a litter. Discuss with your veterinarian the various charges for prenatal and postnatal care for your brood bitch as well as the puppies. All puppies will need first shots and worming, and some breeds require additional procedures such as dewclaw removal or tail docking. Lastly, don't forget advertising costs. Check with local newspapers for their classified rates. If you must run an ad more than once, it can get quite expensive. After you're finished paying these bills, there's not much left in the way of profit.

And that's if the pups are healthy. If there are health complications with the brood bitch or puppies, your small profit can quickly be swallowed up by veterinary expenses. If you don't have a financial cushion in case of medical emergencies, you should certainly think twice about breeding. In any case, it's wise to consult your veterinarian or an experienced breeder about the types of breeding and whelping problems common to your particular breed.

Aside from the desire to make a little money, the reason most people cite for wanting to breed their dog is to give their children a chance to witness the miracle of birth. Although the idea is appealing, it may not be a compelling enough reason to breed a dog. People who sincerely love dogs must be aware of the tremendous canine overpopulation problem in this country. Each year, an estimated 8 to 10 million unwanted dogs and cats are euthanized in America's shelters. Purebred dogs make up an increasingly large percentage of these discarded animals— some shelters report that 30 percent of their dogs are purebreds. Most of these dogs come from backyard, or amateur, breeders who were not aware of the glutted puppy market for their breed or weren't adequately prepared for a litter.

If these figures are uncomfortably high for you as a pet lover, you may want to reconsider breeding your dog. To expose your children to the miracle of birth, show them one of the many nature videos that feature different species birthing and raising their young. Your local library is a great resource.

Before breeding even the most wonderful dog, such as this collie, seriously consider whether you want to add to the millions of dogs who need homes.

Is Your Dog of Breeding Quality?

If you're still enthusiastic about breeding your dog after considering your resources and motives, you'll need to determine honestly whether your pet is of breeding quality. One of the most common misconceptions is that if a dog is registered with the AKC (that is, if he has "papers"), he is guaranteed to be a quality animal. Nothing could be further from the truth. Although there are many fine dogs registered with the AKC, it is just a registry. The only guarantee you get with AKC papers is that the dog is a purebred. But individual purebred dogs vary greatly from litter to litter and within a litter, and not all of them should be bred. Some have faults that are minor and don't detract from the overall beauty of the animal; nevertheless they are undesirable and should not be passed on.

How do you go about deciding if your dog passes muster? The place to start is breed-specific books found in pet stores, book stores, and libraries. These books describe the breed standard: what your dog would look like if he were a perfect example of the breed. The standard gives the ranges of height, weight, and body proportions. Other aspects of the animal

This dog is a good example of the breed standard for the briard.

that are specified are color, markings, length and texture of coat, shape of the head, set of the ears and eyes, eye color, shape of the feet, tail carriage, topline (the visual line along the top of the dog relating the height of the shoulders to the height of the rump), angulation (how much bend in the hind knee, or stifle, is appropriate), bite (how the teeth fit together when the mouth is closed), and gait (style of movement).

All of these elements are important when evaluating your dog for breeding purposes because together they add up to what is called type—the combination that makes a purebred look like the breed he is. No dog is absolutely perfect, but the standard is necessary to ensure the continuation of the purebred dog. To keep the quality of the breed consistent, breeders must "breed for type."

The AKC sells breed videos for most of its recognized breeds. These are an excellent way to study breed standards, and as a bonus you get to see how the breed should move. Dogs who are pigeon-toed or whose hocks bend inward generally do not move properly.

These English cocker spaniels were bred for their gentle, sweet temperaments as well as for conformation.

Going to a dog show is another good way to observe some of the better specimens of your breed. Dog shows are usually advertised in the pet section of the newspaper classifieds. Exhibitors at dog shows often are experienced breeders who would be happy to evaluate your dog for you. They may also be familiar with the individual dogs listed on your dog's pedigree and can give you some information about them. Listen carefully and objectively to the breeder's evaluation. A dog may look good and still have too many faults to be part of a breeding program. The goal of breeding is to improve the stock of purebred dogs; unfortunately, many attractive and good-tempered pets just don't make the grade.

Appearance isn't everything either. Your dog's personality is important to consider as well. While personality varies from one dog to another, it's generally acknowledged that temperament is inherited. Dogs with undesirable traits will pass these traits on to their offspring. Overly aggressive dogs who bite, growl, or intimidate should not be bred, nor should dogs who are excessively nervous or fearful. Nervous dogs often become "fear biters" and can be just as dangerous as overtly aggressive dogs, especially toward children.

All responsible breeders strive to produce even-tempered, tractable dogs, but to be considered breeding quality, your dog also needs to exhibit the traits specific to his breed. Retrievers should retrieve, pointers should point, herding dogs should herd, and so forth. If you are considering breeding one of the working breeds, the dog's innate desire to do what he was bred for should be part of the breeding criteria.

When you've decided that you have a handsome specimen of a breed with a sound temperament, you'll still have one final hurdle before embarking on your breeding program: your pet must be genetically healthy.

Sadly, the majority of purebred dogs are susceptible to a variety of inheritable diseases. Many of these diseases are painful, disabling, and extremely expensive to treat. No one would willingly inflict these diseases on their beloved pet, and the only way to cut down on their incidence is to breed only those dogs who have been screened and certified clear of specific conditions.

Many large dogs such as Labrador retrievers can suffer from hip dysplasia. That is why it is very important to purchase puppies only from responsible breeders who screen for genetic diseases.

Genetic screening has become as important as fitting the standard. Many canine diseases are "silent"—a dog can be asymptomatic for years, and by the time the symptoms emerge, the animal may already have been bred. The only way

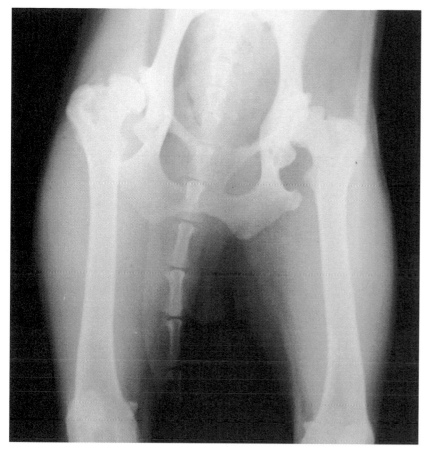

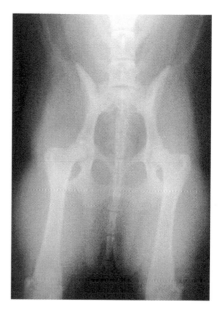

X rays can determine whether a dog has hip dysplasia or other bone and joint problems. The X ray of the dysplastic hip on the left shows how the ball and socket do not fit together properly. The other X ray is a normal hip.

to be sure that your dog does not have a specific condition is to have him screened. Even then, a dog who has been cleared will sometimes produce puppies who have the very conditions the parents have been screened for. When this happens, the dogs should be considered carriers and removed from your breeding program.

X rays reveal most common joint problems. Canine hip dysplasia, a condition in which the ball and socket of the hip joint do not fit together properly, affects larger breeds. This causes deterioration in the joint and painful arthritis. Other common joint conditions are elbow dysplasia, disk problems in the back, and a shoulder condition called osteochondritis dissecans, in which a developing puppy's bone cartilage chips off.

These most common joint problems can be determined through X rays taken by your veterinarian and read by a qualified radiologist. The Orthopedic Foundation for Animals (OFA) is a registry that will read hip, elbow, and shoulder X rays and issue a certificate stating that your dog is clear of these conditions, if he is indeed clear. You will also receive a quality rating ranging from "excellent" to "extremely

Some dogs are genetically susceptible to eye problems. This Yorkshire terrier suffers from cataracts.

dysplastic." Dogs who do not pass should not be bred. X rays cost between $40 and $100 per film, depending upon the weight of the dog. The OFA charges $25 per reading. Ask your veterinarian about exact costs and procedures in your area.

Your dog should also have an eye screening. Many dogs are susceptible to cataracts, progressive retinal atrophy (which leads to blindness), and entropion, where the eyelid rolls inward and ulcerates the eyeball. A qualified veterinary ophthalmologist can perform an eye screening for about $25. If the dog passes the exam, a certificate from the Canine Eye Registry Foundation can be obtained for an additional $7.50. All dogs in a breeding program should have their eyes screened annually. A dog with an inheritable eye disease should not be bred.

Joint and eye problems are only the most common genetic conditions; there are many others that are breed-specific. Part of your research should include asking your veterinarian and experienced breeders about the health problems commonly found in your breed. Pedigrees—the record of your dog's ancestors—can also be somewhat helpful: the newer ones issued by the AKC have "OFA/CERF" listed below the registered name of the dogs who passed the screenings.

The most successful dog breeders combine knowledge, objectivity, and commitment with a little bit of luck to produce healthy, handsome dogs with fine temperaments.

Now that you know what it takes to be a responsible

breeder, you'll want to know the how-to details. It is beyond the scope of this book to go into all the aspects of breeding such as finding a stud dog or brood bitch, mating the dogs, preparing for puppies, neonatal care, and all the types of problems that may develop along the way. But before you decide to become a breeder, it's crucial that you research the subject. A professional breeder can also provide invaluable advice and assistance. In addition to seeking help from vets and breeders, check your pet store and library for books that cover these subjects in detail. Things can go wrong every step of the way, and the more knowledge you have about breeding, the better you'll be able to handle emergencies.

Profile of a Responsible Breeder

🐕 Researches the market before breeding to ensure there will be a reasonable demand for this particular breed of dog; maintains a waiting list of prospective owners if possible

🐕 Has the time, resources, and commitment to give every animal in his or her possession the proper nutrition, exercise, veterinary care, and training that particular breed needs

🐕 Has a thorough understanding of the breed standard and has specific goals for improving the breed

🐕 Performs all necessary health and genetic screening prior to breeding

🐕 Participates in conformation shows, obedience trials, and other dog events to earn titles for his or her dogs for prospective breeding

🐕 Breeds only healthy, sufficiently mature animals in good condition

🐕 Meets or surpasses local kennel licensing requirements

🐕 Screens potential puppy buyers to make sure that new homes provide a good environment and an adequate level of care

🐕 Is willing to assist puppy buyers with advice on the breed and proper care and training

🐕 Is willing to take back or help place in another home a dog from his or her litter if a new owner can no longer keep him

A Dog for All Reasons

9

Now that you have a dog, what can the two of you do together? Will your days be spent turning down dinner invitations because you have to walk the dog? Not at all. Most people are thrilled to discover just how easily their dogs fit into their lives, especially after some basic obedience training.

Dogs accompany their people on sailboats and trains, in convertibles and on river-rafting trips. They are a standard sight at most beaches and parks, playing Frisbee or launching into a lake to retrieve a stick. Hikers take their dogs with them on lengthy backpacking treks (the dogs carry their food in their own backpacks). Toy dogs have been known to take cross-country bicycle tours, securely seated in a cushioned basket on the back of the owner's bike. In France where they have long held a position of great esteem, dogs are welcome guests at most restaurants. While that may never be the case in the U.S., the well-trained dog is usually greeted with delight by the people she meets on her outings.

Many dog owners find themselves drawn to the world of competitions and trials, where the bond between owner and dog is forged by teamwork and the rush of winning an event. Competitions are staged for every kind of dog, from simple conformation and obedience trials to more adventurous contests. Tracking, retrieving, and pointing trials are just a few of the events geared toward hunting dogs. For sight hounds such as Afghans and greyhounds, lure coursing provides the animals an opportunity to race through a field following the ever-changing patterns of a moving lure. Sledding is an age-old sport that can be enjoyed in competitions or simply for the fun of it. Dogs who were born to guard can fulfill their purpose in *schutzhund* competitions, where their ability to find and restrain a "bad guy" is rewarded.

One of the most popular competitions in recent times is flyball, a team sport that's something like a relay race for dogs. The crowds go wild for this event, which has dogs racing over hurdles to catch a ball as it flies from a spring-loaded box, then speeding back over the hurdles to the starting point. It requires real teamwork between dog and handler, and it is perfect for those dogs who can't get enough of chasing balls. Along the same lines, agility trials are an ideal showcase for dogs who love to explore every nook and cranny. The agility course features a wide range of challenges, from A-frames and hurdles to catwalks, seesaws, and tunnels. The dog who gets through the course the fastest wins.

But plenty of dog owners are quite content to develop a quieter comradeship with their pet. For them, the morning and evening walk becomes a much-anticipated part of each day, providing a few moments to unwind and reconnect with life's simple pleasures. Today more than ever, experts are acknowledging the psychological benefits of owning a dog. Dogs are routinely used in pet therapy programs to provide comfort to people who are ill or depressed.

Take her along! Whether you're going to the park, on a bike ride, or to the beach, it's always more fun to take your dog.

People for thousands of years have benefited from the enriching experience of having a dog.

Whatever your reasons for getting a dog, chances are if you research your breed and take the time to make a good match, you'll be surprised and pleased at the added dimension your pet will bring to your life. Over the years, as your dog takes her place in your family albums, you may very well wonder how you ever lived without her.

Travel Tips

Alpo Petfoods and San Diego Zoo goodwill ambassador Joan Embery have collaborated on a free handbook about traveling with pets by car, boat, airplane, and train. *Take Me Along* contains information about hotels, pet containment, overseas travel, and more. To request a handbook, write to *Take Me Along*, Alpo Petfoods, Professional Relations, P.O. Box 25200, Lehigh Valley, PA 18002-5200.

For people planning on taking an airplane trip with their dog, the American Dog Owner's Association booklet *Update: Airplane Transportation* is a must-read. It lists the pet-related safety records of the major airlines, describes the pet storage areas in different types of planes, and tells you how to back up the airline's safety procedures for shipping dogs. The booklet is available for 50¢ from the American Dog Owner's Association, Inc., 1654 Columbia Turnpike, Castleton, NY 12033.

CLUBS AND ORGANIZATIONS

American Kennel Club (AKC)
51 Madison Ave.
New York, NY 10010
(212) 696-8392
All inquiries concerning pedigrees and registration of a dog or litter should be directed to:
American Kennel Club
5580 Centerview Drive
Raleigh, NC 27606
(919) 233-9767

American Humane Association
63 Inverness Dr. East
Englewood, CO 80112
(800) 227-4645

United Kennel Club
100 E. Kilgore Rd.
Kalamazoo, MI 49001-5598
(616) 343-9020

Delta Society
National Headquarters
321 Burnett St.
Renton, WA 98055
(206) 226-7357

Humane Society of the U.S.
2100 L Street, NW
Washington D.C. 20037
(202) 452-1100

4-H Club (Information)
9595 Nelson Rd.
Longmont, CO 80501
(303) 776-4865

Therapy Dogs International
6 Hilltop Road
Mendham, NJ 07945
(201) 543-0989
This organization certifies therapy dogs.

The Dog Museum
1721 S. Mason Road
St. Louis, MO 63131
(314) 821-3647
A large museum, filled with art and much more, celebrating the dog.

Canine Eye Registry Foundation (CERF)
Purdue University
W. Lafayette, IN 47907
(317) 494-8179

Orthopedic Foundation for Animals (OFA)
2300 E. Nifong Blvd.
Columbia, MO 65201-3856
(314) 442-0418

MAGAZINES

Dog Fancy
Dogs USA
Pet Life
AKC Gazette
Dog & Kennel
Dog World
Dogs Today
Your Dog
Puppies USA
Healthy Dogs

VIDEOS AND BOOKS

Note: Many fine pet-related videos and books are published or produced by small companies that may not be distributed in your local video store or bookstore. Dog & Cat Book Catalog, published by Direct Book Service of Wenatchee, Washington, is a good resource for both books and videotapes, and features both popular and hard-to-find titles. To order a catalog, phone (800) 776-2665.

VIDEOS

Dunbar, Ian. *Dr. Ian Dunbar's Sirius Puppy Training Video.*

How You Can Save Your Dog's Life, hosted by Bernadine Cruz, DVM. MediaMax Productions; to order, call (800) 440-8386.

Wilkes, Gary and Pryor, Karen. *Click and Treat Training Kit: Video, Booklet, and Two Clickers.*

BOOKS

Carlson, Delbert G., D.V.M., and Giffin, James M., D.V.M. *Dog Owner's Home Veterinary Handbook.* New York: Howell Book House, 1992.

Christiansen, Bob. *Choosing a Shelter Dog: Complete Guide to Help You Rescue and Rehome a Dog.* Carlsbad, CA: Canine Learning Center, 1995.

DeBitetto, James, D.V.M. *Puppy Owner's Veterinary Care Book.* Howell Book House, 1995.

Delmar, Diana. *The Guilt Free Dog Owner's Guide: Caring for a Dog When You're Short on Time and Space.* Pownal, VT: Storey Communications, 1980.

Kalstone, Shirlee. *How to Housebreak Your Dog in 7 Days.* New York: Bantam, 1985.

Kilcommons, Brian, and Sarah Wilson. *Good Owners, Great Dogs.* New York: Warner Books, 1992.

Lowell, Michele. *Your Purebred Puppy: A Buyer's Guide.* New York: Henry Holt and Co., 1991.

The Monks of New Skete. *How to be Your Dog's Best Friend: A Training Manual for Dog Owners.* Little, Brown, 1978.

Pryor, Karen. *Don't Shoot the Dog! How to Improve Yourself and Others Through Behavioral Training.* New York: Simon and Schuster, 1984.

HOTLINES

The following hotlines are sponsored by both commercial and noncommercial organizations; most offer free telephone consultations, and many offer free written materials as well. Callers pay long-distance charges if the number does not have an 800 area code.

Alpo
(800) 366-6033
Pet nutrition and Alpo product information. 9:00 A.M. to 5:00 P.M. EST, Monday through Friday.

Animal Behavior Helpline
San Francisco ASPCA
(415) 554-3075
Information about behavior of dogs and cats. Messages can be left twenty-four hours a day, seven days a week. Calls returned within twenty-four hours.

Dial-Pet
Chicago Veterinary Medical Association
(630) 844-2862
Offers prerecorded information on a variety of topics regarding domestic animals; caller must have a touch-tone phone to access information. Twenty-four hours a day, seven days a week.

Hill's Pet Nutrition Line
(800) 445-5777
Pet nutrition and Hill's product information. 8:00 A.M. to 6:00 P.M. CST, Monday through Friday.

IAMS Pet Nutrition Hotline
(800) 525-4267, ext. 44
Pet nutrition and care, IAMS product information. 8:00 A.M. to 8:00 P.M. Monday through Saturday.

National Dog Registry
(800) 637-3647
Consultation for lost or found pets, registry, tattooing, assistance in locating lost pets. Twenty-four hours a day, seven days a week.

Petfinders
(800) 666-5678
Assistance in locating lost pets. 9:00 A.M. to 5:00 P.M. EST, Monday through Friday.

Pet Lover's Helpline
(900) 776-0007
A service of the United Pet Clubs of America. Twenty-four hours a day, seven days a week. Charges 97¢ a minute to hear your choice of recorded messages with information about dogs and cats. Free guide to topics is available.

Poison Control Center
(800) 548-2423 or (900) 680-0000
The 800 number is for emergency information on poisoning; callers are charged $30.00 per case. The 900 number is for non-emergency questions; callers pay $20.00 for the first five minutes and $2.95 a minute thereafter. Twenty-four hours a day, seven days a week.

ProPlan
(800) 776-7526, or (800) 835-3323 for hard-of-hearing callers. General information on pet nutrition and ProPlan products. A wealth of free written material is available upon request. 9:00 A.M. to 4:00 P.M., Monday through Friday. CST.

Tree House Animal Foundation
(773) 784-5488 or (773) 784-5605 for hard-of-hearing callers. Free consultation on behavioral problems in dogs and cats. 9:00 A.M. to 5:00 P.M. CST.

❧ ❧ ❧

HELP WITH GRIEVING OVER THE LOSS OF A PET

The following hotlines provide counselors to comfort people who have recently lost a beloved pet.

Pet Loss Support Helpline
Chicago, Illinois
(630) 603-3994

Pet Loss Support Hotline
Davis, California
(916) 752-4200

Pet Loss Support Hotline
Gainesville, Florida
(904) 392-4700, ext. 4080

Pet Loss Support Hotline
Ann Arbor, Michigan
(517) 336-2696

Glossary

angulation: the angle at which a dog's stifle (hind knee) is bent

backyard breeder: an inexperienced dog breeder who is in business to make money rather than improve the breed

breed standard: a set of specifications describing the ideal physical and behavioral attributes of a breed

brood bitch: a female dog who is designated to be bred

conformation: the overall physical traits of a dog that conform to breed standards

crate: a wire or molded plastic container designed to house a pet

dam: the mother of a litter

gait: the way a dog moves when he walks

heat: the estrus cycle of a female dog. Most females go into heat twice a year.

hip dysplasia: a common condition in large dogs in which the ball and socket of the hip joint do not fit together properly

hobby breeder: an experienced dog breeder who strives to improve the breed

neoteny: the selective breeding of dogs to encourage puppylike physical and behavioral characteristics

pedigree: a registry recording a line of ancestors of three generations or more

purebred: a dog bred from members of a recognized strain, without admixture of other blood, over many generations

selective breeding: breeding intended to encourage specific traits such as coat color, docility, or size

sire: the father of a litter

socialization period: the stage in a puppy's life, from roughly three to thirteen weeks, where he establishes social relationships with other dogs and with people

stifle: the hind leg joint, or knee

stud: a male dog intended for breeding purposes

tail carriage: the way in which a dog holds his tail

topline: the visual line along the top of a dog from the shoulders to the rump

type: the combination of physical characteristics that define the way a breed looks

Index